THE CELTIC TWILIGHT

Queen Maeve and Knocknarea

THE
CELTIC TWILIGHT

W. B. Yeats

with an introduction by
Kathleen Raine

illustrated by
Jean Townsend

COLIN SMYTHE
Gerrards Cross 1981

This edition of *The Celtic Twilight* first published in 1981
by Colin Smythe Limited, Gerrards Cross, Buckinghamshire,
England.

British Library Cataloguing in Publication Data

Yeats, W.B.
The Celtic twilight.
1. English literature. Irish authors
I. Title
829'.8'09415   PR8844

ISBN 0-86140-069-0
IBSN 0-86140-070-4 Pbk

Printed in Great Britain by Billing & Sons Ltd.
Guildford, London, Worcester, Oxford

CONTENTS

ILLUSTRATIONS
by Jean Townsend

INTRODUCTION

THE CELTIC TWILIGHT, part chronicle, part auto-
biography, and all drawn from Yeats's early memories
of the west of Ireland, was first published in 1893,
when the poet was twenty-eight. He had already published in
1888 *Fairy and Folk Tale of the Irish Peasantry: Represen-
tative Irish Tales* in 1891, and a year later *Irish Fairy Tales*. All
these involved much reading and were more or less hack work
undertaken for money. But in *The Celtic Twilight* Yeats
writes not from books but from life; memories of things heard,
seen, and felt in his native county Sligo, the home of his
family, that beautiful part of Connaught that lies between
Knoc-na-rea and Ballisodare in the south, Ben Bulben and
Rosses Point in the north. In 1902 he published an enlarged
edition containing additional stories collected in Galway.
Yeats had now met Lady Gregory, and she herself, inspired by
the poet, set about collecting the folk-lore of the neighbourhood of Kiltartan, Coole and Ballylee, where many years later
Yeats was himself to live in the old Norman tower.

The present edition contains the text of the earlier version
(1893) but with the additions of the later stories also—those
dated 1902 in the second edition.

The second edition is undoubtedly the better book;
besides a few minor changes (a little rewriting in the first section, "This Book" and more extensive changes and omissions
in the chapter about AE, "A Visionary") there is much new
material, most of it of a better quality, closer to the people
of Ireland and their world, than any in the first version. It
contained, however, one important section omitted from the

second edition, "The Four Winds of Desire". This is in the nature of a critical essay and although not without interest it is not a first-hand record and this is no doubt why in the second version Yeats substituted the short but very beautiful apology for oral tradition, "By the Roadside". Some of the 1902 material comes from Mary Battle, housekeeper to Yeats's uncle George Pollexfen, who told of her visions of Queen Maeve and her women on Knoc-na-rea; but most he owed to his friendship with Lady Gregory and his visits to County Galway. "Dreams that Have no Moral" was given to him by Lady Gregory herself, who had taken it down from an old man in Gort Workhouse; other sections, like those relating to the memories of the poet Raftery and Mary Hynes were told to Yeats himself, but through Lady Gregory's introduction, and usually in her company. The story of the two souls serving their term in purgatory in a windy bush in County Mayo is a later addition to "Concerning the Nearness Together of Heaven, Earth and Purgatory"—an image Yeats was later to use in *The Dreaming of the Bones*.

The first version, which is mainly a record of Yeats's own memories and conversations and experiments in magic certainly does not show him to be particularly gifted as a collector of folklore. The "Kiltartanese" dialect characteristic of Lady Gregory's writings (and exemplified in "Dreams that have no Moral") has of recent years been much decried by the critics. Doubtless Douglas Hyde's transcriptions and translations of Irish speech are more authentic and less touched up; certainly the artistry of Synge made more memorable use of that speech. Nevertheless Yeats's interest in the speech of the country people, as it developed between the first and second editions of *The Celtic Twilight*, marks an important development also in his development as a poet. That language was not merely a debased dialect of English but an English enriched by the idiom of Gaelic grammar which underlies it; by turns of phrase and turns of thought alien and new, from the standpoint of writers in English, and an undoubted enrichment. It was from the Irish country people that Yeats heard a language purely oral, language as it is for men and women who do not read or write, but speak their words. It was from the son of the farmer who had taught Lady Gregory and Douglas Hyde their Irish grammar that I heard how, many years later, Yeats himself used to walk past that farm along the road between Coole and Ballylee, saying over his poems to himself as he walked and, as the countryman put it, "humming like a swarm of bees". Yeats too had learned to test his poetry by the ear.

Yeats was never himself a folklorist in the sense in which his friend Douglas Hyde was a gatherer of stories, or the Scottish folklorist Campbell, collector of *Tales of the Western Highlands*, or Alexander Carmichael, collector of the *Carmena Gadelica*; but, himself doubtless inspired by these older predecessors, became in his turn an inspirer of others, including the American, W.Y. Evans-Wentz, whose book *The Fairy-faith in Celtic Countries* is dedicated to Yeats and to AE, who had been his guides and advisors when he had visited Ireland in 1909-10. The story of Yeats sending John Millington Synge home to Ireland from Paris to learn his art from the people of the Aran Islands is known to all.

But for Yeats the stories he heard in his boyhood were not folk-lore: they were the stuff of his own daily life, the soil in which his genius was to grow, the source of the themes and symbols of his greatest work. Yeats's family, on both sides, belonged to the Protestant Anglo-Irish; he knew little of the Catholic religion, yet it was above all from the Catholic country-people, tenants or servants of the family, farmers and fishermen, that he derived his first real knowledge and belief in another world: not the Christian religion but the age-old "fairy faith"; which may have been (so argues Evans-Wentz, who most likely took the idea from Yeats) a remote heritage of the religion of the Druids, and is in any case immemorially old. Yeats's father, son of the Rector of Drumcliff, was himself a sceptic and this may have made it easier for his son to follow without conflict on religious grounds his heart, whose "secret fanaticism" led him into the imaginative world of a race whose lives were tinctured by the daily and nightly presence of the supernatural. It was not merely a different set of opinions Yeats discovered in these people but a different awareness, a different mode of consciousness from that of the deist Protestantism or more explicit rationalism of the educated classes.

On an everyday level supernatural events, "the little stitches that join this world and the other", are the experiences of the country-people themselves, for whom the earth is by no means the lifeless material object of scientific knowledge, but populous with lives of many kinds, visible and invisible, beautiful and terrible. A girl in a field close to her home finds herself "astray" out of normal time, in the faery-world where a year is only a moment, or a moment a year. A farmer may meet on the road that terrible beast the Pookah, or be chased by a hairless black pig. Yeats himself, with some cousins, watched strange "lights" coming and going over the site of a former village. Faery-music, rappings and moving objects, "wee folk, good folk, trooping all together" as in William Allingham's poem, besides all the usual ghosts and apparitions whose record is world-wide, were as much part of the life of Sligo as births, marriages, deaths and market-fairs. Whether or not realities of the natural world these were, and remain, realities of the imagination.

The native Irish race inherits, besides, a true mythology. The ancient gods of Ireland still inhabited the great megalithic burial-sites, Aengus of the Birds his Dun at Brugh na Boyne, and other gods at Knowth and elsewhere. The legendary Queen Maeve who led her armies against Ulster's champion Cuchulain is said to be buried under the cairn on the summit of Knoc-na-rea, visible to all Sligo, and to this day unexcavated. Mary Battle, housekeeper to Yeats's uncle George Pollexfen, told how she "was standing at the window looking over to Knoc-na-rea where Queen Maeve is thought to be buried, when she saw, as she told me, 'the finest woman you ever saw travelling right across from the mountain straight to her.' The woman had a sword by her side and a dagger lifted up in her hand, and was dressed in white, with bare arms and feet. She looked strong, but not wicked—that is, not cruel." She was "handsomer than anyone you ever saw". Of others, riding the hills with short dresses and buskins, she said that "there is no such race living now, none so finely proportioned."

Yeats had loved such stories, as child and boy, because they were interwoven with places he knew and loved, places where he fished, collected beetles, or wandered by day or night for the sheer love of his native earth. Ben Bulben "sets the scene" of inner and outer worlds alike; and for childhood these are one and indivisible, as they were for the Irish poor. It was of his own country Yeats was reminded when he came upon boys and girls at a wide space by the road at Kiltartan:

...then some of the men stood up and began to dance, while another lifted the measure they danced to, and then somebody sang *Eiblin a Rúin*, that glad song of meeting which has always moved me more than other songs, because the lover who made it sang it to his sweetheart under the shadow of a mountain I looked at every day through my childhood. The voices melted into the twilight, and were mixed into the trees, and when I thought of the words they too melted away, and were mixed with the generations of men. Now it was a phrase, now it was an attitude of mind, an emotional form, that had carried my memory to older verses, or even to forgotten mythologies. I was carried so far that it was as though I came to one of the four rivers, and followed it under the wall of Paradise to the roots of the trees of knowledge and of life.

Indeed the other world (if not Paradise itself) was near at hand:

A little north of the town of Sligo, on the southern side of Ben Bulben, some hundreds of feet above the plain, is a small white square in the limestone. No mortal has ever touched it with his hand; no sheep or goat has ever browsed grass beside it. There is no more inaccessible place on earth, and few more encircled by awe to the deep considering. It is the door of fairyland. In the middle of the night it swings open, and the unearthly troop rushes

out. All night the gay rabble sweep to and fro across
the land.

It is to be understood that in Celtic countries the faery
world is dreaded; not far removed from the country of
the dead, or that world itself, beautiful as it may be, it
is "the world's bane". The passage continues:

> ...the unearthly troop do not always return empty-
> handed. Sometimes a new-wed bride or a new-born baby
> goes with them into their mountains; the door swings to
> behind; and the new-born or new-wed moves thenceforth
> in the bloodless land of Faery; happy enough, but doomed
> to melt out at the last judgement like bright vapour, for
> the soul cannot live without sorrow.

This theme, common both in Ireland and in Scotland gave
Yeats the matter of several poems and his early play, *The
Land of Heart's Desire*. *The Host of the Air* is a ballad
conceived and written much in the spirit of the narrators
from whom he heard the story; but in the play, as in the
poem *The Stolen Child*, the deep attraction the "other"
world exerted upon Yeats is already clear:

> Come, faeries, take me out of this dull world,
> For I would ride with you upon the wind
> And dance upon the mountains like a flame.

More terribly, more profoundly, the theme is used again
in *The Only Jealousy of Emer*; in which Cuchulain is drawn
away from the world by the faery-woman, Fand, whose
attraction had already captured him in an earlier play,
At the Hawk's Well. Emer wins Cuchulain back from death
by renouncing his love. The chorus, in *At the Hawk's Well*,
recoil from the superhuman world that draws Cuchulain,
as it drew Yeats, with irresistible attraction:

> Come to me, human faces,
> Familiar memories;
> I have found hateful eyes
> Among the desolate places,
> Unfaltering, unmoistened eyes.

...
'The man that I praise',
Cries out the empty well,
'Lives all his days
Where a hand on the bell
Can call the milch cows
To the comfortable door of his house.
Who but an idiot would praise
Dry stones in a well?'

That question remained, for Yeats, open to the end; Plato's question, "For who knows whether to live be not to die, and to die to live?" The gods, in any case, are immortal:

Time drops in decay
Like a candle burnt out,
And the mountains and woods
Have their day, have their day,
Not one in the rout
Of the fire-born moods
Shall pass away.

(The first draft of this poem was prefaced to both editions; it is much inferior, but the phrase in l. 5, "the kindly old rout", closer to the folk-material which is the poet's inspiration.)

That world of memories of which *The Celtic Twilight* is the record was the more passionately loved because Yeats spent his school years in the London suburb of Bedford Park, and Sligo took on the colouring of his dreams; and he longed to have even one sod of Sligo turf that could give reality to his memories. It was the sight of a window-display in Fleet Street that was the occasion of Yeats's writing the poem *The Lake Isle of Innisfree*—a ping-pong ball balanced upon a little jet of water. The reality of his early attempt to live on that isle had been less fortunate—a sleepless night on a rock in fear of being chased away by the woodranger, "I came home unimaginably tired and sleepy having walked some thirty miles partly over rough and boggy ground. For months

13

afterwards if I alluded to my walk my uncle's general servant
... would go into fits of laughter." Perhaps the sense of exile
is the strongest of all poetic urges, since it compels us to
re-create for ourselves the lost country; which carries in it
always in some measure the symbol of lost Paradise. So, as
with Horace's *fons Bandusiae* or Wordsworth's or Beatrix
Potter's Lake District, or Israel's or any other Holy Land, it is
in exile that Yeats's memories were to undergo that transmutation that is generated in the space between desire and
fulfilment. That Paradise must always be a state of being,
of imaginative consciousness, which is natural to childhood,
and to which we all seek to return, or to attain; a timeless
"eternity" which a few mystics attain and poets glimpse
afar off. If Yeats's master Blake was such a mystic, Yeats
was such a poet. By the good fortune which at once gave
him, and withheld from him throughout his unhappy school-
boy years in London, County Sligo, the country denied
him in time was restored to him in the imagination of the
poet.

And yet the real Ireland (if that is the word—for some
might consider the Ireland of the travelling scholars, the
saints and the political exiles, or of the self-banished exile
James Joyce, of all those "wild geese" who have given to
"holy Ireland" its imaginative identity, the more real) never
became for Yeats so remote as to lose its clear and distinct
outline, or for its people to pale into ghosts. He returned for
all his holidays to stay with grandparents and cousins, often
enough for love and memory to be renewed, and was absent
for long enough for transmutation of the actual into the
imagined to be accomplished. Sligo gave him, therefore,
images which were to become also symbols without ever
losing anything of their concreteness of "a local habitation
and a name". In *The Celtic Twilight* and in his other early
writings, *Stories of Red Hanrahan* and the rest—we already
find most of those themes in a form relatively untransmuted,
although already illuminated by the light of imagination. In
his latest, grandest and most symbolically resonant verse we
find still the same images, the same names. The ghosts of

Dermot and Dervorgilla seen by Red Hanrahan give Yeats
the theme of *The Dreaming of the Bones*; Baile and Ailinn,
Cuchulain and Fand, Cruachan's windy plain and the well
whose waters ebb and flow near the hill called *Slieve do
ain* (the mountain of the two birds) are places of the real
world raised by Yeats into places of the imagination. The
megalithic warrior whose bones were found in a tomb near
Sligo, guards *The Black Tower*:

> There in the tomb stand the dead upright
> But the winds come up from the shore:
> They shake when the winds roar,
> Old bones upon the mountain shake.

Even that resounding line

> That dolphin-torn, that gong-tormented sea

from *Byzantium* describes the way west-of-Ireland fishermen
attract the fish by the beating of a gong. Ben Bulben, first
and last, "sets the scene".

Thus the raw material of Yeats's poetry is taken to a far
greater degree than for most poets of the imagination, not from
literature or from introspection but from life. He was of course
widely and deeply read in the literature and philosophy of all
cultures; his work is permeated with the thought of Plato,
Plotinus and the Upanishads. But when we read his poetic and
dramatic works we could hardly guess that Yeats lived more
in England than in Ireland and spent much time in France.

Yeats built upon the foundation of his earliest love, but
the choice was also deliberate. We can only guess at the kind
of poet he might have become, but for that deliberate choice,
from some early work later suppressed. In an essay on
Ireland and the Arts Yeats recalls a time when he was
"without any decided impulse to one thing more than
another, and especially to those who are convinced, as I was
convinced, that art is tribeless, nationless, a blossom gathered
in No Man's Land." Such is *Mosada*, a dramatic fragment set
in Moorish Spain, and that other early poem Gerard Manley
Hopkins called "a strained and unworkable allegory about a
young man and a sphinx on a rock in the sea (how did they
get there? what did they eat?) and so on: people think such

criticisms very prosaic; but commonsense is never out of place anywhere, neither on Parnassus nor on Tabor nor on the Mount where our Lord preached." (Letter to Coventry Patmore, November 7th 1886)

Yeats was to reach for himself the same conclusion:

When I first wrote I went here and there for my subjects as my reading led me and preferred to all countries Arcadia and the India of romance, but presently I convinced myself for such reasons as those in *Ireland and the Arts*, that I should never go for the scenery of a poem to any country but my own, and I think that I shall hold that conviction to the end.

This resolution he kept; and in so doing became not merely a poet of talent but the voice of the imagination of Ireland. As a boy he had listened to the voice of that imagination spoken in "the desolate places" by the poor and dispossessed and illiterate; as a mature poet he made that voice heard throughout the world. In the same essay he had written:

The Greeks, the only perfect artists of the world, looked within their own borders, and we, like them, have a history fuller than any in modern history of imaginative events; and legends which surpass, as I think, all legends but theirs in wild beauty, and in our land, as in theirs, there is no river or mountain that is not associated in the memory with some event or legend.... I would have Ireland recreate the ancient arts, the arts as they were understood in Judaea, in India, in Scandinavia, in Greece and Rome, in every ancient land; as they were understood when they moved a whole people and not a few people who have grown up in a leisured class and made this understanding their business.

"Have not all races had their first unity from a mythology that marries them to rock and hill?" Yeats asked.

If Yeats's first intention was to strengthen his own poetry that intention had soon become a much greater one, to create "an Irish literature which, though made by many minds, would seem the work of a single mind, and turn our places of beauty or legendary association into holy symbols."

Introduction

Whereas an English poet writing at the end of the nine-teenth century must have felt himself overshadowed by the great tradition of English literature and English culture, for an Irish poet there was at that time little to build on. There was the oral tradition of the Irish poor, and an ancient litera-ture written in a language now spoken only by a largely illiterate class; and there was a totally unrelated Anglo-Irish culture belonging to Yeats's own class, the Protestant ascen-dancy, whose great names—Burke and Grattan, Swift and Goldsmith and Berkeley—were unknown to the Gaelic tradition. In *Four Years* (1887-1891) Yeats tells how he had realized that he must build a new tradition; "there was no help for it, seeing that my country was not born at all." He succeeded, in his poetry, in accomplishing what history itself had hitherto failed to bring about, in uniting the culture of the Anglo-Irish—of Yeats and his friends, Lady Gregory and John Millington Synge and Maude Gonne and all those others among his contemporaries and fellow-countrymen whom his poetry has immortalised and his example inspired —names he has made a part of Ireland's inheritance, united with that other tradition, of Mary Battle and Biddy Early and all the "henwives and queer old men" who told him stories. In retrospect it looks as if Ireland had already possessed that "unity of being" which comes from "some inherited subject-matter known to the whole people"; but that is an optical illusion, for it was Yeats himself, and the literary movement he led and inspired, the national theatre he created, that revived a dying tradition and united the shattered fragments into "a symbolical, a mythological coherence." The tradition of "dark Raftery" and O'Carolan, last of the bards, had dwindled to little more than a legend and the oral tradition of a poor and despised peasantry, that three generations would have sufficed to make irrecoverable; as has now come about in neighbouring Scotland.

In his purpose so to "deepen the political passion of the nation, that all, artist and poet, craftsman and day-labourer would accept a common design" so that "Perhaps even those images, once created and associated with river and mountain, might move of themselves and with some powerful, even turbulent life", Yeats was later to wonder if he had been even too successful, and to ask himself

> Did that poem of mine send out
> Certain men the English shot?

—and

> When Pearse summoned Cuchulain to his side
> What stalked through the Post-office?

—scene of the Easter rising, commemorated by the statue of Cuchulain by Yeats's fellow art-student Sheppard. These poetic images had indeed stirred with turbulent life. Yeats quotes some words of Oscar Wilde who, speaking of Hamlet, had said "the world has become sad because a puppet was melancholy." He discovered for himself the power of poetic symbol to alter the course of a nation's life.

But if Yeats's intentions were political they were so in Plato's sense; not the pragmatist's "art of the possible" but a society grounded in the first principles of spiritual tradition. For him the arts were

> ...almost an infallible Church of poetic tradition, of a fardel of stories, and of personages, and of emotions, inseparable from their first expression, passed on from generation to generation by poets and painters with some help from philosophers and theologians. I wished for a world where I could discover this tradition perpetually.
> ...I had even created a dogma: 'Because these imaginary people are created out of the deepest instinct of man, to be his measure and his norm, whatever I can imagine those mouths speaking may be the nearest I can go to truth'.

Far from making a religion of "art", Yeats followed Blake (and also Plato) in demanding that the arts should be the expression of the deepest spiritual truth. It is Blake's religion of the Imagination; who had written

> As all men are alike (tho' infinitely various), So all Religions etc, as all similars, have one source.
> The true Man is the source, he being the Poetic Genius.

* * * * *

It was of such aspiring ends that *The Celtic Twilight* is the modest beginning. There is, in these gleanings and reflections of the young poet a quality of simplicity, of innocence. There is in them nothing of the amused detachment of the collector of "folklore", still less of the unamused detachment of the anthropologist. There had been plenty of nineteenth century writers about the Irish peasantry who made of "Paddy" and his absurdities a laughing-stock. Instead it was Yeats himself who was to become a laughing-stock for just that imaginative sympathy in which lies the genius of the true poet. It is his own life that he records. In County Sligo he discovered the map of the territory of his own imagination, bounded by its contours in hill and wood, wind and weather, bird and beast.

"I have been" he wrote "at no pains to separate my own beliefs from those of the peasantry, but have rather let man and woman, ghouls and faeries, go their way unoffended or defended by any argument of mine. The things a man has heard and seen are the threads of life."

In Ireland (so he wrote in his essay *Ireland and the Arts*) the poets will find "two passions ready to their hands, love of the Unseen Life and love of country". The two are inseparable among the country people and are so in Yeats; inseparable but not indistinguishable. The bardic tradition of Ireland is above all historical. The bardic poets—the ollaves —belonged to the courts of the Irish kings, and their task was to exalt those kings and to celebrate and commit to the memory of the people the memories of great deeds, the magnificence of men and the beauty of women. To receive "a bad press" from the bards could spell disaster. In *The King's Threshold* Yeats affirms the office and the dignity of the bard. O'Carolan, last of the bards, was attached to the household of O'Conor Don at Clonalis in Roscommon, where his harp is kept in honour by the last of the line of those hereditary High Kings for whom the poet and harper sang, composed, and played. The bard is the custodian of the historic identity of a nation, and to the last tattered relics of

19

the Irish nation to whom Yeats listened the memory of "dark" (that is, blind) Raftery was dear. It was in Gort Workhouse that Yeats heard an old man describe the poet: "He was a big man, and his songs have gone through the whole world. I remember him well. He had a voice like the wind." An old woman of Ballylee remotely recalled the rôle of the bard when she said of Raftery

'If you treated him well he'd praise you, but if you did not he'd fault you in Irish. He was the greatest poet in Ireland, and he'd make a song about that bush if he chanced to stand under it. There was a bush he stood under in the rain, and he made verses praising it, and then when the water came through he made verses dispraising it.' She then sang the poem to a friend and to myself in Irish, and every word was audible and expressive.

Raftery died in a leaky cottage where the neighbours remembered that "all night long a light was streaming up to heaven from the roof of the house where he lay, and that was the angels who were with him...they gave that honour to him because he was so good a poet, and sang such religious songs." No less remembered was Mary Hynes, the woman Raftery celebrated in his poems. She too lived at Ballylee; and Yeats remembers:

An old man brought me a little way from the mill and the castle, and down a long narrow boreen that was nearly lost in brambles and sloe bushes and he said 'That is the little old fountain of the house, but the rest of it is taken for building walls, and the goats have ate those bushes that are growing over there till they have got cranky, and they won't grow any more. They say she was the handsomest girl in Ireland.'

So she may have been; but it is oral tradition, "the book of the people", that has made her so. An old woman remembered:

As many as eleven men asked her in marriage in one day but she wouldn't have any of them. There was a lot of men up beyond Kilbecan one night sitting together drinking and talked of her, and one of them got up and set out to go to Ballylee and see her; but Cloon Bog was open then, and when he came to it he fell into the water, and they found him dead there in the morning. She died of the fever that was before the famine.

So the imagination of the people transmutes fact into legend; and that legend, recorded in *The Celtic Twilight* just as Yeats heard it, he raised to a greater grandeur in *The Tower*. It was Raftery's rhymes that had given its power to the beauty of Mary Hynes:

> And certain men, being maddened by those rhymes,
> Or else by toasting her a score of times,
> Rose from the table and declared it right
> To test their fancy by their sight;
> But they mistook the brightness of the moon
> For the prosaic light of day—
> Music had driven their wits astray—
> And one was drowned in the great bog of Cloone.

And Yeats goes on to compare the blind Irish bard with Homer:

> Strange, but the man who made the song was blind;
> Yet, now I have considered it, I find
> That nothing strange; the tragedy began
> With Homer that was a blind man
> And Helen has all living hearts betrayed.

Beauty is a quality of the imagination, not of fact; and Yeats found in the West of Ireland a world like that of Homer, "sweetest of singers" whose island home was "rocky Chios". But before Yeats none of his race or class had recognised that in the Irish peasantry ("their" tenants) the Homeric world lived on; in men like Paddy Flynn, "a little bright-eyed old man who lived in a leaky one-roomed cabin in the village of Ballisodare." Yet such people, tinkers and beggars and the unregarded poor, were the true heirs of the Ireland of the kings and the bards. Paddy Flynn was "a great teller of tales" who

...knew how to empty heaven, hell and purgatory, faeryland and earth to people his stories. He did not live in a shrunken world, but knew no less ample circumstances than did Homer himself. Perhaps the Gaelic people shall by his like bring back the ancient simplicity and amplitude of imagination.

The prophecies of great poets are themselves events that have already happened; Yeats was a bard in the old sense, giving Ireland's story its place in the record of the imagination of the world. And those two qualities he admired—simplicity and amplitude—are surely the marks of his own greatest poetry.

But Yeats avoided the fallacy—if fallacy it was—of Wordsworth's search to imitate the speech of the common man in a mode which made some of his *Lyrical Ballads* simple to the point of absurdity. After a few early attempts in ballad style made in his first resolve "to write always out of the common thought of the people" Yeats quickly realised that it is not from "the market-place, the songs of the workmen" that the thought of the people is to be discovered, but in "some Ogham on a stone, or the conversation of a countryman who knows more of the Boar without Bristles than of the daily paper." (The boar without bristles doubtless is a remote echo of the shape-changing Druids who turned themselves into swine, and a relation of the Truich Truith, the wild boar hunted in the Mabinogion in neighbouring Wales.) Nothing, Yeats understood, is more venerable than the records of unwritten tradition; and in *The Celtic Twilight* he wrote

…though one can know but little of their ascent, one knows that they ascend like mediaeval genealogies through unbroken dignities to the beginning of the world. Folk art is, indeed, the oldest of the aristocracies of thought, and because it refuses what is passing and trivial, the merely clever and pretty, as certainly as the vulgar and insincere, and because it has gathered into itself the simplest and most unforgettable thoughts of the generations, it is the soil where all great art is rooted.

He found in such men as the "roaring tinker" the highest of

aristocracy, divine descent; whose name, Mannion, comes
from Mannanan, the sea-god of the Celts:

> All Mannions come from Mannanan,
> Though rich on every shore
> He never lay behind four walls
> He had such character,
> Nor ever made an iron red
> Nor soldered pot or pan.

Indeed it is from the masks of his "henwives and queer
old men" that Yeats speaks his profoundest thoughts; nor
was this a mere literary device, for from them he learned
his deepest wisdom. There is in *The Celtic Twilight* a fairy-
tale of nearly twenty pages transcribed in a workhouse by
"a friend" (Lady Gregory) who had

> ...found the old people cold and wretched, 'like flies in
> winter', she said: but they forgot the cold when they
> began to talk. A man had just left them who had played
> cards in a rath with the people of faery, who had played
> 'very fair'; and one old man had seen an enchanted black
> pig one night, and there were two old people my friend
> had heard quarrelling as to whether Raftery or Callanan
> was the better poet.

The faery-cards Yeats used as the opening theme of his
Stories of Red Hanrahan; and it was to the poor and despised
that Hanrahan in his turn was to sing his songs and tell his
stories. Hanrahan met on the road to Collooney an old
woman who was surely in the later poems to become Crazy
Jane the beggar-woman in the dignity of her dreams and
memories, an embodiment of Ireland's Cathleen ni Houlihan,
in her guise of the "Poor Old Woman" the *shan van vocht*;
as she appears in Yeats's play that bears her name.

> ...one Margaret Rooney, a woman he used to know in
> Munster when he was a young man. She had no good
> name at that time, and it was the priest routed her out
> at last. He knew her by her walk and by the colour of
> her eyes, and by a way she had of putting back the hair

off her face with her left hand. She had been wandering about, she said, selling herrings and the like, and now she was going back to Sligo to the place in the Burrough where she was living with another woman, Mary Gillis, who had much the same story as herself. She would be well pleased, she said, if he would come and stop in the house with them, and he singing his songs to the bacachs and blind men and fiddlers of the Burrough...and all the bacachs and poor men that heard him would give him a share of their own earnings for his stories and his songs while he was with them, and would carry his name into all the parishes of Ireland.

(The Burrough was Sligo's disreputable district; it lay just outside the town on the road that runs north towards Drum-cliff and Rosses; the Burrough has since been destroyed and rebuilt.) Hanrahan stays with these people, outcasts of an ancient race, who hold the bard still in honour; and like Raftery's, "the sound of his voice was like the wind in a lonely place." He sings Yeats's poem to "Cathleen, the daughter of Houlihan";

...while he was singing his voice began to break, and tears come rolling down his cheeks and Margaret Rooney put down her face into her hands and began to cry along with him. Then a blind beggar by the fire shook his rags with a sob and after that there was no one left of them all but cried tears down.

And this story is echoed (with no doubt a memory also of Mary Battle's visions of Queen Maeve and the Sidhe riding from Knoc-na-rea and Ben Bulben) in one of his late poems, *Crazy Jane on the Mountain*; she too having been routed out by the priests:

> I am tired of cursing the Bishop
> (Said Crazy Jane)
> Nine books or nine hats
> Would not make him a man.
> I have found something worse
> To meditate on.

A king had some beautiful cousins,
But where are they gone?
Battered to death in a cellar,
And he stuck to his throne.
Last night I lay on the mountain
(Said Crazy Jane)
There in a two-horsed carriage
That on two wheels ran
Great-bladdered Emer sat,
Her violent man
Cuchulain sat at her side;
Thereupon,
Propped upon my two knees,
I kissed a stone;
I lay stretched out in the dirt
And I cried tears down.

The king and his "beautiful cousins" refers to Conchubar and the Sons of Usna, whom he treacherously murdered because of Deirdre, who had preferred Naoise to himself.

* * * * *

As for the Irish passion for "the Unseen Life", Yeats discovered in a culture which literacy and the mass media had not yet touched the traces of a primordial tradition as old as the world itself, and in no way differing from the learned traditions of Platonism and the Upanishads. It was, he believed, Western materialism that is a provincial heresy from this universal knowledge, whose end he foresaw and did all in his considerable power to bring about. When in 1920 Lady Gregory published her *Visions and Beliefs in the West of Ireland* Yeats contributed an important essay entitled *Swedenborg, Mediums and the Desolate Places*.

He had over the years read deeply in those Neoplatonic and Far Eastern books whose philosophy is grounded in the premise that mind, or spirit, is the ground of what we call reality. He had also made practical studies of the Western

25

esoteric tradition of magic, and serious and highly critical experiments in psychical research. He had now come to hold a "doctrine of souls", whose first traces he had discovered in his Sligo boyhood. Yeats had found that most of the phenomena of séances and other phenomena studied by psychical research had their counterpart in the folk-beliefs of "the desolate places".

> I was amused to make Holloway interpret Aran, and constantly comparing my discoveries with what I have learned of mediaeval tradition among my fellow students with the reveries of a Neoplatonist, of a seventeenth-century Platonist, of Paracelsus or a Japanese poet.

In the writings of Swedenborg (known to him as a boy, but now re-examined in a more scientific spirit) he found doctrines which gave coherence to the knowledge which, over the years, he had gathered in areas of study superficially remote from one another, and confirmation of much he had himself seen and heard. In the light of Plato and Plotinus, Porphyry and the Upanishads, he was able to see Swedenborg himself in the larger context of a universal tradition of spiritual knowledge. He wrote of Swedenborg's system according to which after death

> ...the soul lives a life so like that of the world that it may not even believe that it has died... It is the other world of the early races, of those whose dead are in the rath or the faery hill, of all who see no place of reward or punishment, but a continuation of this life, with cattle and sheep, markets and war. This earth-resembling life is the creation of the image-making power of the mind, plucked naked from the body, and mainly of the images in the memory.

This was a world he had known from childhood; all he had lacked was a philosophy to give it meaning.

This is the world to which the great Islamic scholar Henry Corbin has given the name of the "Imaginal" (in contrast to the pejorative "imaginary")—the *mundus imaginalis* or *imaginatio vera*, whose "place" is the mind itself. It is the earth of *Hûrqalyâ* described by the Islamic mystical theologians as the "real" earth of the soul, as this world is real to the body. Corbin writes:

L'éveil à la conscience de Hûrqalyâ annonce un nouveau mode de l'âme avec l'étendue, avec tout ce qui est corporel et spatial, relation qui ne peut être un rapport de contenu et contenant. Le mode de vision de la Terre est le mode même de la vision de l'âme, le vision en laquelle elle se perçoit; ce peut être son paradis, et ce peut être son enfer. (The awakening of the awareness of Hûrqalyâ preludes a new mode of relationship with extension, with whatever is corporeal and spatial, a relationship which cannot be that of contained and containing. The earthly mode of vision is the mode also of the soul's vision, the vision in which the soul perceives itself; it may be its paradise, or it may be its hell.)

It is into this "terre de vérité", the world of its own truth, that the soul "plucked naked from its body" is "resurrected" at death; an intermediate world of imaginal forms.

...c'est le monde par lequel se corporalisent les esprits et par lequel se spiritualisent les corps. Ce monde intermédiatrice n'est accessible qu'à l'Imagination active, à la fois instauratrice de son univers propre et transmutatrice des données sensibles en symboles. (...it is the world by whose means spirits are corporealised and bodies spiritualised. This intermediate world is accessible only to the active Imagination, at the same time establishing it in its proper universe, and transmuting sense-date into symbols.)

Corbin himself greatly admired Yeats's two masters, Blake, and Swedenborg of whom Blake was himself a follower; but was not, so far as I know, acquainted with Yeats's remarkable essay in which he could have found rich confirmation of what he had himself found in the learned tradition of Iranian mystical theology.

So heaven and hell are built always anew and in hell or heaven all do what they please and all are surrounded by scenes and circumstances which are the expression of their natures and the creation of their thought.

Such are the little hurley-players watched by some workmen in a field; the huntsmen and the fairy hounds, the

27

buskined women who ride from Ben Bulben's white door. All live in that world the Iranian mystics call *Hûrqalyâ*, the Irish country people the world of faery, and Blake the Imagination. "It is the real world" Blake had written "into which we shall all go after the death of this mortal body." It is in this world where thoughts are things that the poets of the Imagination —*Imaginatio vera*—find their "images of wonder".

In many of his early poems—*The Happy Townland*, *The Man who Dreamed of Faery-land*, *The Host of the Air*—Yeats describes this world of images where the simple dreams of the poor are realities:

> Boughs have their fruit and blossom
> At all times of the year;
> Rivers are running over
> With red beer and brown beer.
> An old man plays bagpipes
> In a golden and silver wood;
> Queens, their eyes blue like ice
> Are dancing in a crowd.

Here Yeats is putting into verse the material of folk-themes much as he found it. In his latest and grandest work the same material was to be wrought into poetry of unsurpassed depth of meaning. In *The Dreaming of the Bones* the unlaid ghosts of Dermot and Dervorgilla, whom Red Hanrahan had seen on Ben Bulben, become the theme of a play of the supernatural based on the Nô theatre of Japan; whose themes are usually enacted in the "twilight" between inner and outer worlds. In this play Yeats has used many details taken from *The Celtic Twilight*, like the souls who do penance in a thorn-bush; and so in *Purgatory*, last and greatest of his plays of the supernatural. In *Swedenborg, Mediums and the Desolate Places* Yeats writes of a Nô play in which a priest marries the ghosts of two country lovers long dead, and of the same story (it is told by Lady Gregory), of lovers who came to a priest for marriage after death, from the Aran islands. He did not himself write a play upon this theme; but in one of his last collections, *Supernatural Songs*, *Ribh at the Tomb of*

Baile and Ailinn recalls the story known since boyhood of two lovers who died in sorrow each thinking the other dead. In no poem has Yeats given more profound and complete expression to his own and ancient Ireland's doctrine of souls. Dead lovers and holy man have alike in their spiritual bodies attained their "celestial earth":

> Here in the pitch-dark atmosphere above
> The trembling of the apple and the yew,
> Here on the anniversary of their death,
> The anniversary of their first embrace,
> Those lovers purified by tragedy
> Hurry into each other's arms; these eyes,
> By water, herb and solitary prayer
> Made aquiline, are open to that light,'
> Though somewhat broken by the leaves, that light
> Lies in a circle on the grass; therein
> I turn the pages of my holy book.

Kathleen Raine

Time drops in decay
Like a candle burnt out,
And the mountains and woods
Have their day, have their day;
But, kindly old rout
Of the fire-born moods,
You pass not away.

THE HOST

The host is riding from Knocknarea,
  And over the grave of Clooth-na-bare;
  Caolte tossing his burning hair,
And Niam calling, 'Away, come away;

'And brood no more where the fire is bright,
  Filling thy heart with a mortal dream;
  For breasts are heaving and eyes a-gleam:
Away, come away, to the dim twilight.

'Arms are a-waving and lips apart;
  And if any gaze on our rushing band,
  We come between him and the deed of his hand,
We come between him and the hope of his heart.'

The host is rushing 'twixt night and day;
  And where is there hope or deed as fair?
  Caolte tossing his burning hair,
And Niam calling, 'Away, come away.'

THIS BOOK

I HAVE desired, like any artist, to create a little world out of the beautiful, pleasant, and significant things of this marred and clumsy world, and to show in a vision something of the face of Ireland to any of my own people who would look where I bid them. I have therefore written down accurately and candidly much that I have heard and seen, and, except by way of commentary, nothing that I have merely imagined. I have, however, been at no pains to separate my own beliefs from those of the peasantry, but have rather let my men and women, dhouls and faeries, go their way unoffended or defended by any argument of mine. The things a man has heard and seen are threads of life, and if he pull them carefully from the confused distaff of memory, any who will can weave them into whatever garments of belief please them best. I too have woven my garment like another, but I shall try to keep warm in it, and shall be well content if it do not unbecome me.

Hope and Memory have one daughter and her name is Art, and she has built her dwelling far from the desperate field where men hang out their garments upon forked boughs to be banners of battle. O beloved daughter of Hope and Memory, be with me for a little.   1893.

II

I have added a few more chapters in the manner of the old ones, and would have added others, but one loses, as one grows older, something of the lightness of one's dreams; one begins to take life up in both hands, and to care more for the fruit than the flower, and that is no great loss perhaps. In these new chapters, as in the old ones, I have invented nothing but my comments and one or two deceitful sentences that may keep some poor story-teller's commerce with the devil and his angels, or the like, from being known among his neighbours. I shall publish in a little while a big book about the commonwealth of faery, and shall try to make it systematical and learned enough to buy pardon for this handful of dreams.   1902.

W. B. YEATS.

A TELLER OF TALES

MANY of the tales in this book were told me by one Paddy Flynn, a little bright-eyed old man, who lived in a leaky and one-roomed cabin in the village of Ballisodare, which is, he was wont to say, 'the most gentle' —whereby he meant faery—'place in the whole of County Sligo. Others hold it, however, but second to Drumcliff and Dromahair. The first time I saw him he was bent above the fire with a can of mushrooms at his side; the next time he was asleep under a hedge, smiling in his sleep. He was indeed always cheerful, though I thought I could see in his eyes (swift as the eyes of a rabbit, when they peered out of their wrinkled holes) a melancholy which was wellnigh a portion of their joy; the visionary melancholy of purely instinctive natures and of all animals.

And yet there was much in his life to depress him, for in the triple solitude of age, eccentricity, and deafness, he went about much pestered by children. It was for this very reason perhaps that he ever recommended mirth and hopefulness. He was fond, for instance, of telling how Columcille cheered up his mother. 'How are you today, mother?' said the saint. 'Worse,' replied the mother. 'May you be worse to-morrow,' said the saint. The next day Columcille came again, and exactly the same conversation took place, but the third day the mother said, 'Better, thank God.' And the saint replied, 'May you be better to-morrow.' He was fond too of telling how the Judge smiles at the Last Day alike when he rewards the good and condemns the lost to unceasing flames. He had many strange sights to keep him

cheerful or to make him sad. I asked him had he ever seen
the faeries, and got the reply, 'Am I not annoyed with them?'
I asked too if he had ever seen the banshee. 'I have seen it,'
he said, 'down there by the water, batting the river with its
hands.'

BELIEF AND UNBELIEF

THERE are some doubters even in the western villages. One woman told me last Christmas that she did not believe either in Hell or in ghosts. Hell was an invention got up by the priest to keep people good; and ghosts would not be permitted, she held, to go 'trapsin' about the earth' at their own free will; 'but there are faeries and little leprechauns, and water-horses, and fallen angels.' I have met also a man with a Mohawk Indian tattooed upon his arm, who held exactly similar beliefs and unbeliefs. No matter what one doubts, one never doubts the faeries, for, as the man with the Mohawk Indian on his arm said, 'they stand to reason.'

A little girl who was at service in the village of Grange, close under the seaward slopes of Ben Bulben, suddenly disappeared one night about three years ago. There was at once great excitement in the neighbourhood, because it was rumoured that the faeries had taken her. A villager was said to have long struggled to hold her from them, but at last they prevailed, and he found nothing in his hands but a broom-stick. The local constable was applied to, and he at once instituted a house-to-house search, and at the same time advised the people to burn all the *bucalauns* (ragweed) on the field she vanished from, because *bucalauns* are sacred to the faeries. They spent the whole night burning them, the constable repeating spells the while. In the morning the little girl was found wandering in the field. She said the faeries had taken her away a great distance, riding on a faery horse. At last she saw a big river, and the man who had tried to keep her from being carried off was drifting down it—such are the topsyturvydoms of faery glamour—in a cockle-shell. On the way her companions had mentioned the names of several people who were to die shortly in the village.

MORTAL HELP

ONE hears in the old poems of men taken away to help the gods in a battle, and Cuchulain won the goddess Fand for a while, by helping her married sister and her sister's husband to overthrow another nation of the Land of Promise. I have been told, too, that the people of Faery cannot even play at hurley unless they have on either side some mortal, whose body—or whatever has been put in its place, as the storyteller would say—is asleep at home. Without mortal help they are shadowy and cannot even strike the balls. One day I was walking over some marshy land in Galway with a friend when we found an old, hard-featured man digging a ditch. My friend had heard that this man had seen a wonderful sight of some kind, and at last we got the story out of him. When he was a boy he was working one day with about thirty men and women and boys. They were beyond Tuam and not far from Knocknagur. Presently they saw, all thirty of them, and at a distance of about half a mile, some hundred and fifty of the people of Faery. There were two of them, he said, in dark clothes like people of our own time, who stood about a hundred yards from one another, but the others wore clothes of all colours, 'bracket' or chequered, and some had red waistcoats.

He could not see what they were doing, but all might have been playing hurley, for 'they looked as if it was that.' Sometimes they would vanish, and then he 'would almost swear' they came back out of the bodies of the two men in dark clothes. These two men were of the size of living men, but the others were small. He saw them for about half an hour, and then the old man he and those about him were working for took up a whip and said, 'Get on, get on, or we will have no work done!' I asked if he saw the faeries too. 'O yes, but he did not want work he was paying wages for to be neglected.' He made everybody work so hard that nobody saw what happened to the faeries.

A VISIONARY

A YOUNG man came to see me at my lodgings the other night, and began to talk of the making of the earth and the heavens and much else. I questioned him about his life and doings. He had written many poems and painted many mystical designs since we met last, but latterly had neither written nor painted, for his whole heart was set upon making his character vigorous and calm, and the emotional life of the artist was bad for him, he feared. He recited his poems readily, however. He had them all in his memory. Some indeed had never been written down. Suddenly it seemed to me that he was peering about him a little eagerly. 'Do you see anything, X——?' I said. 'A shining, winged woman, covered by her long hair, is standing near the doorway,' he answered, or some such words. 'Is it the influence of some living person who thinks of us, and whose thoughts appear to us in that symbolic form?' I said; for I am well instructed in the ways of the visionaries and in the fashion of their speech. 'No,' he replied; 'for if it were the thoughts of a person who is alive I should feel the living influence in my living body, and my heart would beat and my breath would fail. It is a spirit. It is some one who is dead or who has never lived.'

I asked what he was doing, and found he was clerk in a large shop. His pleasure, however, was to wander about upon the hills, talking to half-mad and visionary peasants, or to persuade queer and conscience-stricken persons to deliver up the keeping of their troubles into his care. Another night, when I was with him in his own lodging, more than one turned up to talk over their beliefs and disbeliefs, and sun them as it were in the subtle light of his mind. Sometimes visions come to him as he talks with them, and he is rumoured to have told divers people true matters of their past days and distant friends, and left them hushed with dread of their strange teacher, who seems scarce more than a boy, and is so much more subtle than the oldest among them.

The poetry he recited me was full of his nature and his visions. Sometimes it told of other lives he believes himself to have lived in other centuries, sometimes of people he had talked to, revealing them to their own minds. I told him I would write an article upon him and it, and was told in turn that I might do so if I did not mention his name, for he wished to be always 'unknown, obscure, impersonal.' Next day a bundle of his poems arrived, and with them a note in these words: 'Here are copies of verses you said you liked. I do not think I could ever write or paint any more. I prepare myself for a cycle of other activities in some other life. I will make rigid my roots and branches. It is not now my turn to burst into leaves and flowers.'

The poems were all endeavours to capture some high, impalpable mood in a net of obscure images. There were fine passages in all, but these were often embedded in thoughts which have evidently a special value to his mind, but are to other men the counters of an unknown coinage. At other times the beauty of the thought was obscured by careless writing as though he had suddenly doubted if writing was not a foolish labour. He had frequently illustrated his verses with drawings, in which an imperfect anatomy did not altogether smother a beauty of feeling. The faeries in whom he believes have given him many subjects, notably Thomas of Ercildoune sitting motionless in the twilight while a young and beautiful creature leans softly out the shadow and whispers in his ear. He had delighted above all in strong effects of colour: spirits who have upon their heads instead of hair the feathers of peacocks; a phantom reaching from a swirl of flame towards a star; a spirit passing with a globe of iridescent crystal —symbol of the soul—half shut within his hand. But always

41

under this largess of colour lay some appeal to human sympathy. This appeal draws to him all those who, like himself, seek for illumination or else mourn for a joy that has gone. One of these especially comes to mind. A winter or two ago he spent much of the night walking up and down upon the mountain talking to an old peasant who, dumb to most men, poured out his cares for him. Both were unhappy: X——because he had then first decided that art and poetry were not for him, and the old peasant because his life was ebbing out with no achievement remaining and no hope left him. The peasant was wandering in his mind with prolonged sorrow. Once he burst out with, 'God possesses the heavens —God possesses the heavens—but He covets the world'; and once he lamented that his old neighbours were gone, and that all had forgotten him: they used to draw a chair to the fire for him in every cabin, and now they said, 'Who is that old fellow there?' 'The fret' (Irish for doom) 'is over me,' he repeated, and then went on to talk once more of God and Heaven. More than once also he said, waving his arm towards the mountain, 'Only myself knows what happened under the thorn-tree forty years ago'; and as he said it the tears upon his face glistened in the moonlight.

VILLAGE GHOSTS

THE ancient map-makers wrote across unexplored regions, 'Here are lions.' Across the villages of fishermen and turners of the earth, so different are these from us, we can write but one line that is certain, 'Here are ghosts.'

My ghosts inhabit the village of H——, in Leinster. History has in no manner been burdened by this ancient village, with its crooked lanes, its old abbey churchyard full of long grass, its green background of small fir-trees, and its quay, where lie a few tarry fishing-luggers. In the annals of entomology it is well known. For a small bay lies westward a little, where he who watches night after night may see a certain rare moth fluttering along the edge of the tide, just at the end of evening or the beginning of dawn. A hundred years ago it was carried here from Italy by smugglers in a cargo of silks and laces. If the moth-hunter would throw down his net, and go hunting for ghost tales or tales of those children of Lilith we call faeries, he would have need for far less patience.

To approach the village at night a timid man requires great strategy. A man was once heard complaining, 'By the Cross of Jesus! how shall I go? If I pass by the hill of Dunboy old Captain Burney may look out on me. If I go round by the water, and up by the steps, there is the headless one and another on the quays, and a new one under the old churchyard wall. If I go right round the other way, Mrs. Stewart is appearing at Hillside Gate, and the Devil himself is in the Hospital Lane.'

I never heard which spirit he braved, but feel sure it was not the one in the Hospital Lane. In cholera times a shed had been there set up to receive patients. When the need had gone

43

The white cat

44

by, it was pulled down, but ever since the ground where it stood has broken out in ghosts and demons and faeries. There is a farmer at H——, Paddy B—— by name, a man of great strength, and a teetotaller. His wife and sister-in-law, musing on his great strength, often wonder what he would do if he drank. One night, when passing through the Hospital Lane, he saw what he supposed at first to be a tame rabbit; after a little he found that it was a white cat. When he came near, the creature slowly began to swell larger and larger, and as it grew he felt his own strength ebbing away, as though it were sucked out of him. He turned and ran.

By the Hospital Lane goes the 'Faeries Path'. Every evening they travel from the hill to the sea, from the sea to the hill. At the sea end of their path stands a cottage. One night Mrs. Arbunathy, who lived there, left her door open, as she was expecting her son. Her husband was asleep by the fire; a tall man came in and sat beside him. After he had been sitting there for a while, the woman said, 'In the name of God, who are you?' He got up and went out, saying 'Never leave door open at this hour, or evil may come to you.' She woke her husband and told him. 'One of the Good People has been with us,' said he.

Probably the man braved Mrs. Stewart at Hillside Gate. When she lived she was the wife of the Protestant clergyman. 'Her ghost was never known to harm any one,' say the village people; 'it is only doing penance upon the earth.' Not far from Hillside Gate, where she haunted, appeared for a short time a much more remarkable spirit. Its haunt was the boreen, a green lane leading from the western end of the village. In a cottage at the village end of the boreen lived a house-painter, Jim Montgomery, and his wife. They had several children. He was a little dandy, and came of a higher class than his neighbours. His wife was a very big woman; but he, who had been expelled from the village choir for drink, gave her a beating one day. Her sister heard of it, and came and took down one of the window shutters—Montgomery was neat about everything, and had shutters on the outside of every window—and beat him with it, being big and strong

45

like her sister. He threatened to prosecute her; she answered that she would break every bone in his body if he did. She never spoke to her sister again, because she had allowed herself to be beaten by so small a man. Jim Montgomery grew worse and worse: his wife before long had not enough to eat, but she would tell no one, for she was very proud. Often, too, she would have no fire on a cold night. If any neighbours came in she would say she had let the fire out because she was just going to bed. The people often heard her husband beating her, but she never told any one. She got very thin. At last one Saturday there was no food in the house for herself and the children. She could bear it no longer, and went to the priest and asked him for some money. He gave her thirty shillings. Her husband met her, and took the money, and beat her. On the following Monday she got very ill, and sent for a Mrs. Kelly. Mrs. Kelly, as soon as she saw her, said, 'My woman, you are dying,' and sent for the priest and the doctor. She died in an hour. After her death, as Montgomery neglected the children, the landlord had them taken to the workhouse. A few nights after they had gone, Mrs. Kelly was going home through the boreen when the ghost of Mrs. Montgomery appeared and followed her. It did not leave her until she reached her own house. She told the priest, Father S——, a noted antiquarian, and could not get him to believe her. A few nights afterwards Mrs. Kelly again met the spirit in the same place. She was in too great terror to go the whole way, but stopped at a neighbour's cottage midway, and asked them to let her in. They answered they were going to bed. She cried out, 'In the name of God let me in, or I will break open the door.' They opened, and so she escaped from the ghost. Next day she told the priest again. This time he believed, and said it would follow her until she spoke to it.

She met the spirit a third time in the boreen. She asked what kept it from its rest. The spirit said that its children must be taken from the workhouse, for none of its relations were ever there before, and that three masses were to be said for the repose of its soul. 'If my husband does not believe you,' she said, 'show him that,' and touched Mrs. Kelly's

wrist with three fingers. The places where they touched
swelled up and blackened. She then vanished. For a time
Montgomery would not believe that his wife had appeared.
'She would not show herself to Mrs. Kelly,' he said—'she with
respectable people to appear to.' He was convinced by the
three marks, and the children were taken from the workhouse. The priest said the masses, and the shade must have
been at rest, for it has not since appeared. Some time afterwards Jim Montgomery died in the workhouse, having come
to great poverty through drink.

I know some who believe they have seen the headless ghost
upon the quay, and one who, when he passes the old cemetery wall at night, sees a woman with white borders to her
cap* creep out and follow him. The apparition only leaves
him at his own door. The villagers imagine that she follows
him to avenge some wrong. 'I will haunt you when I die' is a
favourite threat. His wife was once half scared to death by
what she considers a demon in the shape of a dog.

These are a few of the open-air spirits; the more domestic
of their tribe gather within-doors, plentiful as swallows under
southern eaves.

One night a Mrs. Nolan was watching by her dying child in
Fluddy's Lane. Suddenly there was a sound of knocking
heard at the door. She did not open, fearing it was some
unhuman thing that knocked. The knocking ceased. After a
little the front door and then the back door were burst open,
and closed again. Her husband went to see what was wrong.
He found both doors bolted. The child died. The doors were
again opened and closed as before. Then Mrs. Nolan remembered that she had forgotten to leave window or door open,
as the custom is, for the departure of the soul. These strange
openings and closings and knockings were warnings and
reminders from the spirits who attend the dying.

The house ghost is usually a harmless and well-meaning

* I wonder why she had white borders to her cap. The old Mayo
woman, who has told me so many tales, has told me that her brother-in-
law saw 'a woman with white borders to her cap going round the stacks
in a field, and soon after he got a hurt, and he died in six months.'

creature. It is put up with as long as possible. It brings good luck to those who live with it. I remember two children who slept with their mother and sisters and brothers in one small room. In the room was also a ghost. They sold herrings in the Dublin streets, and did not mind the ghost much, because they knew they would always sell their fish easily while they slept in the 'ha'nted' room.

I have some acquaintance among the ghost-seers of western villages. The Connacht tales are very different from those of Leinster. These H—— spirits have a gloomy, matter-of-fact way with them. They come to announce a death, to fulfil some obligation, to revenge a wrong, to pay their bills even—as did a fisherman's daughter the other day—and then hasten to their rest. All things they do decently and in order. It is demons, and not ghosts, that transform themselves into white cats or black dogs. The people who tell the tales are poor, serious-minded fishing-people, who find in the doings of the ghosts the fascination of fear. In the western tales is a whimsical grace, a curious extravagance. The people who recount them live in the most wild and beautiful scenery, under a sky ever loaded and fantastic with flying clouds. They are farmers and labourers, who do a little fishing now and then. They do not fear the spirits too much to feel an artistic and humorous pleasure in their doings. The ghosts themselves share their hilarity. In one western town, on whose deserted wharf the grass grows, these spirits have so much vigour, I have been told, that, when a misbeliever ventured to sleep in a haunted house, they flung him through the window, and his bed after him. In the surrounding villages they adopt strange disguises. A dead old gentleman steals the cabbages of his own garden in the shape of a large rabbit. A wicked sea-captain stayed for years inside the plaster of a cottage wall, in the shape of a snipe, making the most horrible noises. He was only dislodged when the wall was broken down; then out of the solid plaster the snipe rushed away whistling.

'DUST HATH CLOSED HELEN'S EYE'

I HAVE been lately to a little group of houses, not many enough to be called a village, in the barony of Kiltartan in County Galway, whose name, Ballylee, is known through all the west of Ireland. There is the old square castle,* Ballylee, inhabited by a farmer and his wife, and a cottage where their daughter and their son-in-law live, and a little mill with an old miller, and old ash-trees throwing green shadows upon a little river and great stepping-stones. I went there two or three times last year to talk to the miller about Biddy Early, a wise woman that lived in Clare some years ago, and about her saying, 'There is a cure for all evil between the two mill-wheels of Ballylee,' and to find out from him or another whether she meant the moss between the running waters or some other herb. I have been there this summer, and I shall be there again before it is autumn, because Mary Hynes, a beautiful woman whose name is still a wonder by turf fires, died there sixty years ago; for our feet would linger where beauty has lived its life of sorrow to make us understand that it is not of the world. An old man brought me a little way from the mill and the castle, and down a long, narrow boreen that was nearly lost in brambles and sloe-bushes, and he said, 'That is the little old foundation of the house, but the most of it is taken for building walls, and the goats have ate those bushes that are growing over it till they've got cranky, and they won't grow any more. They say she was the handsomest girl in

* Ballylee Castle, or Thoor Ballylee, as I have named it to escape from the too magnificent word 'castle', is now my property, and I spend my summers or some part of them there. (1924.)

49

Ireland, her skin was like dribbled snow'—he meant driven snow, perhaps—'and she had blushes in her cheeks. She had five handsome brothers, but all are gone now!' I talked to him about a poem in Irish, Raftery, a famous poet, made about her, and how it said, 'There is a strong cellar in Ballylee.' He said the strong cellar was the great hole where the river sank underground, and he brought me to a deep pool, where an otter hurried away under a grey boulder, and told me that many fish came up out of the dark water at early morning 'to taste the fresh water coming down from the hills.'

I first heard of the poem from an old woman who lives about two miles farther up the river, and who remembers Raftery and Mary Hynes. She says, 'I never saw anybody so handsome as she was, and I never will till I die,' and that he was nearly blind, and had 'no way of living but to go round and to mark some house to go to, and then all the neighbours would gather to hear. If you treated him well he'd praise you, but if you did not, he'd fault you in Irish. He was the greatest poet in Ireland, and he'd make a song about that bush if he chanced to stand under it. There was a bush he stood under from the rain, and he made verses praising it, and then when the water came through he made verses dispraising it.' She sang the poem to a friend and to myself in Irish, and every word was audible and expressive, as the words in a song were always, as I think, before music grew too proud to be the garment of words, flowing and changing with the flowing and changing of their energies. The poem is not as natural as the best Irish poetry of the last century, for the thoughts are arranged in a too obviously traditional form, so the old poor half-blind man who made it has to speak as if he were a rich farmer offering the best of everything to the woman he loves, but it has naïve and tender phrases. The friend that was with me has made some of the translation, but some of it has been made by the country-people themselves. I think it has more of the simplicity of the Irish verses than one finds in most translations.

Going to Mass by the will of God,
The day came wet and the wind rose;
I met Mary Hynes at the cross of Kiltartan,
And I fell in love with her then and there.

I spoke to her kind and mannerly,
As by report was her own way;
And she said, 'Raftery, my mind is easy,
You may come to-day to Ballylee.'

When I heard her offer I did not linger,
When her talk went to my heart my heart rose.
We had only to go across the three fields,
We had daylight with us to Ballylee.

The table was laid with glasses and a quart measure,
She had fair hair, and she sitting beside me;
And she said, 'Drink, Raftery, and a hundred welcomes,
There is a strong cellar in Ballylee.'

O star of light and O sun in harvest,
O amber hair, O my share of the world,
Will you come with me upon Sunday
Till we agree together before all the people?

I would not grudge you a song every Sunday evening,
Punch on the table, or wine if you would drink it,
But, O King of Glory, dry the roads before me
Till I find the way to Ballylee.

There is sweet air on the side of the hill
When you are looking down upon Ballylee;
When you are walking in the valley picking nuts and
    blackberries,
There is music of the birds in it and music of the Sidhe.

What is the worth of greatness till you have the light
Of the flower of the branch that is by your side?
There is no god to deny it or to try and hide it,
She is the sun in the heavens who wounded my heart.

There was no part of Ireland I did not travel,
From the rivers to the tops of the mountains,
To the edge of Lough Greine whose mouth is hidden,
And I saw no beauty but was behind hers.

Her hair was shining and her brows were shining too;
Her face was like herself, her mouth pleasant and sweet.
She is the pride, and I give her the branch,
She is the shining flower of Ballylee.

It is Mary Hynes, the calm and easy woman,
Has beauty in her mind and in her face,
If a hundred clerks were gathered together,
They could not write down a half of her ways.

An old weaver, whose son is supposed to go away among the Sidhe (the faeries) at night, says, 'Mary Hynes was the most beautiful thing ever made. My mother used to tell me about her, for she'd be at every hurling, and wherever she was she was dressed in white. As many as eleven men asked her in marriage in one day, but she wouldn't have any of them. There was a lot of men up beyond Kilbecanty one night sitting together drinking, and talking of her, and one of them got up and set out to go to Ballylee and see her; but Cloone Bog was open then, and when he came to it he fell into the water, and they found him dead there in the morning. She died of the fever that was before the famine.' Another old man says he was only a child when he saw her, but he remembered that 'the strongest man that was among us, one John Madden, got his death of the head of her, cold he got crossing rivers in the night-time to get to Ballylee.' This is perhaps the man the other remembered, for tradition gives the one thing many shapes. There is an old woman who remembers her, at Derrybrien among the Echtge hills, a vast desolate place, which has changed little since the old poem said, 'the stag upon the cold summit of Echtge hears the cry of the wolves,' but still mindful of many poems and of the dignity of ancient speech. She says, 'The sun and the moon never shone on anybody so handsome, and her skin was so white that it looked blue, and she had two little blushes on her cheeks.' And an old wrinkled woman who lives close by Ballylee, and has told me many tales of the Sidhe, says, 'I often saw Mary Hynes, she was handsome indeed. She had two bunches of curls beside her cheeks, and they were the colour of silver. I saw Mary Molloy that was drowned in the river beyond, and Mary Guthrie that was in Ardrahan, but she took the sway of them both, a very comely creature. I was at her wake too—she had seen too much of the world. She was a kind creature. One day I was coming home through that field beyond, and I was tired, and who should come out but the Floisin Glegeal (the shining flower), and she gave me a glass of new milk.' This old woman meant no more than some beautiful bright colour by the colour of silver, for though I knew an old man—he is dead now—who thought she might know 'the cure for all the evils in the world,' that the Sidhe knew, she has seen too little gold to know its colour. But a man by the shore at Kinvara, who is too young to remember Mary Hynes, says, 'Everybody says there is no one at all to be seen now so handsome; it is said she had beautiful hair, the colour of gold. She was poor, but her clothes every day were the same as Sunday, she had such neatness. And if she went to any kind of a meeting, they would all be killing one another for a sight of her, and there was a great many in love with her, but she died young. It is said that no one that has a song made about them will ever live long.'

Those who are much admired are, it is held, taken by the Sidhe, who can use ungoverned feeling for their own ends, so that a father, as an old herb-doctor told me once, may give his child into their hands, or a husband his wife. The admired and desired are only safe if one says 'God bless them' when one's eyes are upon them. The old woman that sang the song thinks, too, that Mary Hynes was 'taken', as the phrase is, 'for they have taken many that are not handsome, and why would they not take her? And people came from all parts to look at her, and maybe there were some that did not say "God bless her".' An old man who lives by the sea at Duras has as little doubt that she was taken, 'for there are some living yet can remember her coming to the pattern* there

* A 'pattern', or 'patron', is a festival in honour of a saint.

beyond, and she was said to be the handsomest girl in Ireland.' She died young because the gods loved her, for the Sidhe are the gods, and it may be that the old saying, which we forget to understand literally, meant her manner of death in old times. These poor countrymen and countrywomen in their beliefs, and in their emotions, are many years nearer to that old Greek world, that set beauty beside the fountain of things, than are our men of learning. She 'had seen too much of the world'; but these old men and women, when they tell of her, blame another and not her, and though they can be hard, they grow gentle as the old men of Troy grew gentle when Helen passed by on the walls.

The poet who helped her to so much fame has himself a great fame throughout the west of Ireland. Some think that Raftery was half blind, and say, 'I saw Raftery, a dark man, but he had sight enough to see her,' or the like, but some think he was wholly blind, as he may have been at the end of his life. Fable makes all things perfect in their kind, and her blind people must never look on the world and the sun. I asked a man I met one day, when I was looking for a pool *na mna Sidhe* where women of Faery have been seen, how Raftery could have admired Mary Hynes so much if he had been altogether blind. He said, 'I think Raftery was altogether blind, but those that are blind have a way of seeing things, and have the power to know more, and to feel more, and to do more, and to guess more than those that have their sight, and a certain wit and a certain wisdom is given to them.' Everybody, indeed, will tell you that he was very wise, for was he not not only blind but a poet? The weaver, whose words about Mary Hynes I have already given, says, 'His poetry was the gift of the Almighty, for there are three things that are the gift of the Almighty —poetry and dancing and principles. That is why in the old times an ignorant man coming down from the hillside would be better behaved and have better learning than a man with education you'd meet now, for they got it from God'; and a man at Coole says, 'When he put his finger to one part of his head, everything would come to him as if it was written

54

in a book'; and an old pensioner at Kiltartan says, 'He was standing under a bush one time, and he talked to it, and it answered him back in Irish. Some say it was the bush that spoke, but it must have been an enchanted voice in it, and it gave him the knowledge of all the things of the world. The bush withered up afterwards, and it is to be seen on the roadside now between this and Rahasine.' There is a poem of his about a bush, which I have never seen, and it may have come out of the cauldron of Fable in this shape.

A friend of mine met a man once who had been with him when he died, but the people say that he died alone, and one Maurteen Gillane told Dr. Hyde that all night long a light was seen streaming up to heaven from the roof of the house where he lay, and 'that was the angels who were with him'; and all night long there was a great light in the hovel, 'and that was the angels who were waking him. They gave that honour to him because he was so good a poet, and sang such religious songs.' It may be that in a few years Fable, who changes mortalities to immortalities in her cauldron, will have changed Mary Hynes and Raftery to perfect symbols of the sorrow of beauty and of the magnificence and penury of dreams.

1900

II

When I was in a northern town a while ago I had a long talk with a man who had lived in a neighbouring country district when he was a boy. He told me that when a very beautiful girl was born in a family that had not been noted for good looks, her beauty was thought to have come from the Sidhe, and to bring misfortune with it. He went over the names of several beautiful girls that he had known, and said that beauty had never brought happiness to anybody. It was a thing, he said, to be proud of and afraid of. I wish I had written out his words at the time, for they were more picturesque than my memory of them.

1902

A KNIGHT OF THE SHEEP

AWAY to the north of Ben Bulben and Cope's mountain lives 'a strong farmer', a knight of the sheep they would have called him in the Gaelic days. Proud of his descent from one of the most fighting clans of the Middle Ages, he is a man of force alike in his words and in his deeds. There is but one man that swears like him, and this man lives far away upon the mountain. 'Father in Heaven, what have I done to deserve this?' he says when he has lost his pipe; and no man but he who lives on the mountain can rival his language on a fair-day over a bargain.

One day I was dining with him when the servant-maid announced a certain Mr. O'Donnell. A sudden silence fell upon the old man and upon his two daughters. At last the eldest daughter said somewhat severely to her father, 'Go and ask him to come in and dine.' The old man went out, and then came in looking greatly relieved, and said, 'He says he will not dine with us.' 'Go out,' said the daughter, 'and ask him into the back parlour, and give him some whiskey.' Her father, who had just finished his dinner, obeyed sullenly, and I heard the door of the back parlour—a little room where the daughters sat and sewed during the evening—shut to behind the men. The daughter then turned to me and said, 'Mr. O'Donnell is the tax-gatherer, and last year he raised our taxes, and my father was very angry, and when he came, brought him into the dairy, and sent the dairy-woman away on a message, and then swore at him a great deal. "I will teach you, sir," O'Donnell replied, "that the law can protect its officers"; but my father reminded him that he had no witness. At last my father got tired, and sorry too, and said he would show him a short way home. When they were half-way to the main road they came on a man of my father's who was ploughing, and this somehow brought back remembrance of the wrong. He sent the man away on a message, and began to swear at the tax-gatherer again. When I heard of it I was disgusted that he should have made such a fuss over a miserable creature like O'Donnell; and when I heard a few weeks ago that O'Donnell's only son had died and left him heart-broken, I resolved to make my father be kind to him next time he came.'

She then went out to see a neighbour, and I sauntered towards the back parlour. When I came to the door I heard angry voices inside. The two men were evidently getting on to the tax again, for I could hear them bandying figures to and fro. I opened the door; at the sight of my face the farmer was reminded of his peaceful intentions, and asked me if I knew where the whiskey was. I had seen him put it into the cupboard, and was able therefore to find it and get it out, looking at the thin, grief-struck face of the tax-gatherer. He was rather older than my friend, and very much more feeble and worn, and of a very different type. He was not like him, a robust, successful man, but rather one of those whose feet find no resting-place upon the earth. 'You are doubtless of the stock of the old O'Donnells,' I said. 'I know well the hole in the river where their treasure lies buried under the guard of a serpent with many heads.' 'Yes, sir,' he replied, 'I am the last of a line of princes.'

We then fell to talking of many commonplace things, and when at last the gaunt old tax-gatherer got up to go, my friend said, 'I hope we will a glass together next year.' 'No, no,' was the answer, 'I shall be dead next year.' 'I too have lost sons,' said the other, in quite a gentle voice. 'But your sons were not like my son.' And then the two men parted, with an angry flush and bitter hearts, and had I not cast between them some common words or other, might not have parted, but have fallen rather into an angry discussion of the value of their dead sons.

The knight of the sheep would have had the victory. He was indeed but once beaten; and this is his tale of how it was. He and some farm-hands were playing at cards in a small cabin that stood against the end of a big barn. A wicked woman had once lived in this cabin. Suddenly one of the players threw down an ace and began to swear without any cause. His swearing was so dreadful that the others stood up, and my friend said, 'All is not right here; there is a spirit in him.' They ran to the door that led into the barn to get away as quickly as possible. The wooden bolt would not move, so the knight of the sheep took a saw which stood against the wall near at hand, and sawed through the bolt, and at once the door flew open with a bang, as though some one had been holding it, and they fled through.

AN ENDURING HEART

ONE DAY a friend of mine was making a sketch of my knight of the sheep. The old man's daughter was sitting by, and, when the conversation drifted to love and love-making, she said, 'O, father, tell him about your love affair.' The old man took his pipe out of his mouth and said, 'Nobody ever marries the woman he loves,' and then, with a chuckle, 'There were fifteen of them I liked better than the woman I married,' and he repeated many women's names. He went on to tell how when he was a lad he had worked for his grandfather, his mother's father, and was called (my friend has forgotten why) by his grandfather's name, which we will say was Doran. He had a great friend, whom I shall call John Byrne; and one day he and his friend went to Queenstown to await an emigrant ship, that was to take John Byrne to America. When they were walking along the quay, they saw a girl sitting on a seat, crying miserably, and two men standing up in front of her quarrelling with one another. Doran said, 'I think I know what is wrong. *That* man will be her brother, and *that* man will be her lover, and the brother is sending her to America to get her away from the lover. How she is crying! but I think I could console her myself.' Presently the lover and brother went away, and Doran began to walk up and down before her, saying, 'Mild weather, Miss,' or the like. She answered him in a little while, and the three began to talk together. The emigrant ship did not arrive for some days; and the three drove about on outside cars very innocently and happily, seeing everything that was to be seen. When at last the ship came, and Doran had to break it to her that he was not going to America, she cried more after him than after the first lover. Doran whispered to Byrne as he went aboard ship, 'Now, Byrne, I don't grudge her to you, but don't marry young.'

When the story got to this, the farmer's daughter joined in mockingly with, 'I suppose you said that for Byrne's good, father.' But the old man insisted that he *had* said it for Byrne's good; and went on to tell how, when he got a letter telling of Byrne's engagement to the girl, he wrote him the same advice. Years passed by, and he heard nothing; and though he was now married, he could not keep from wondering what she was doing. At last he went to America to find out, and though he asked many people for tidings, he could get none. More years went by, and his wife was dead, and he well on in years, and a rich farmer with not a few great matters on his hands. He found an excuse in some vague business to go out to America again, and to begin his search again. One day he fell into talk with an Irishman in a railway carriage, and asked him, as his way was, about emigrants from this place and that, and at last, 'Did you ever hear of the miller's daughter from Innis Rath?' and he named the woman he was looking for. 'O yes.' said the other, 'she is married to a friend of mine, John MacEwing. She lives at such-and-such a street in Chicago.' Doran went to Chicago and knocked at her door. She opened the door herself, and was 'not a bit changed.' He gave her his real name, which he had taken again after his grandfather's death, and the name of the man he had met in the train. She did not recognise him, but asked him to stay to dinner, saying that her husband would be glad to meet anybody who knew that old friend of his. They talked of many things, but for all their talk, I do not know why, and perhaps he did not know why, he never told her who he was. At dinner he asked her about Byrne, and she put her head down on the table and began to cry, and she cried so he was afraid her husband might be angry. He was afraid to ask what had happened to Byrne, and left soon after, never to see her again.

When the old man had finished the story, he said, 'Tell that to Mr. Yeats, he will make a poem about it, perhaps.' But the daughter said, 'O no, father. Nobody could make a poem about a woman like that.' Alas! I never made the poem, perhaps because my own heart, which has loved Helen and all the lovely and fickle women of the world, would be too sore. There are things it is well not to ponder over too much, things that bare words are the best suited for.

1902.

THE SORCERERS

IN Ireland we hear but little of the darker powers,* and come across any who have seen them even more rarely, for the imagination of the people dwells rather upon the fantastic and capricious, and fantasy and caprice would lose the freedom which is their breath of life, were they to unite them either with evil or with good. I have indeed come across very few persons in Ireland who try to communicate with evil powers, and the few I have met keep their purpose and practice wholly hidden from those among whom they live. They are mainly small clerks, and meet for the purpose of their art in a room hung with black hangings, but in what town that room is I shall not say. They would not admit me into this room, but finding me not altogether ignorant of the arcane science, showed elsewhere what they could do. 'Come to us,' said their leader, 'and we will show you spirits who will talk to you face to face, and in shapes as solid and heavy as our own.'

I had been talking of the power of communicating in states of trance with the angelical and faery beings—the children of the day and of the twilight—and he had been contending that we should only believe in what we can see and feel when in our ordinary everyday state of mind. 'Yes,' I said, 'I will come to you,' or some such words; 'but I will not permit myself to become entranced, and

---

* I know better now. We have the dark powers much more than I thought, but not as much as the Scottish, and yet I think the imagination of the people does dwell chiefly upon the fantastic and capricious.

will therefore know whether these shapes you talk of are any the more to be touched and felt by the ordinary senses than are those I talk of.' I was not denying the power of other beings to take upon themselves a clothing of mortal substance, but only that simple invocations, such as he spoke of, seemed unlikely to do more than cast the mind into trance.

'But,' he said, 'we have seen them move the furniture hither and thither, and they go at our bidding, and help or harm people who know nothing of them.' I am not giving the exact words, but as accurately as I can the substance of our talk.

On the night arranged I turned up about eight, and found the leader sitting alone in almost total darkness in a small back room. He was dressed in a black gown, like an inquisitor's dress in an old drawing, that left nothing of him visible except his eyes, which peered out through two small round holes. Upon the table in front of him was a brass dish of burning herbs, a large bowl, a skull covered with painted symbols, two crossed daggers, and certain implements, whose use I failed to discover, shaped like quern-stones. I also put on a black gown, and remember that it did not fit perfectly, and that it interfered with my movements considerably. The sorcerer then took a black cock out of a basket, and cut its throat with one of the daggers, letting the blood fall into the large bowl. He opened a book and began an invocation, which was neither English nor Irish, and had a deep guttural sound. Before he had finished, another of the sorcerers, a man of about twenty-five, came in, and having put on a black gown also, seated himself at my left hand. I had the invoker directly in front of me, and soon began to find his eyes, which glittered through the small holes in his hood, affecting me in a curious way. I struggled hard against their influence, and my head began to ache. The invocation continued, and nothing happened for the first few minutes. Then the invoker got up and extinguished the light in the hall, so that no glimmer might come through the slit under the door. There was now no light except from the herbs on the brass dish, and no sound except from the deep guttural murmur of the invocation.

Presently the man at my left swayed himself about, and cried out, 'O God! O God!' I asked him what ailed him, but he did not know he had spoken. A moment after he said he could see a great serpent moving about the room, and became considerably excited. I saw nothing with any definite shape, but thought that black clouds were forming about me. I felt I must fall into a trance if I did not struggle against it, and that the influence which was causing this trance was out of harmony with itself, in other words, evil. After a struggle I got rid of the black clouds, and was able to observe with my ordinary senses again. The two sorcerers now began to see black and white columns moving about the room, and finally a man in a monk's habit, and they became greatly puzzled because I did not see these things also, for to them they were as solid as the table before them. The invoker appeared to be gradually increasing in power, and I began to feel as if a tide of darkness was pouring from him and concentrating itself about me; and now too I noticed that the man on my left hand had passed into a death-like trance. With a last great effort I drove off the black clouds; but feeling them to be the only shapes I should see without passing into a trance, and having no great love for them, I asked for lights, and after the needful exorcism returned to the ordinary world.

I said to the more powerful of the two sorcerers, 'What would happen if one of your spirits had overpowered me?' 'You would go out of this room,' he answered, 'with his character added to your own.' I asked about the origin of his sorcery, but got little of importance, except that he had learned it from his father, and that one word which he had repeated several times was Arabic. He would not tell me more, for he had, it appeared, taken a vow of secrecy.

THE DEVIL

MY old Mayo woman told me one day that something very bad had come down the road and gone into the house opposite, and though she would not say what it was, I knew quite well. Another day she told me of two friends of hers who had been made love to by one whom they believed to be the Devil. One of them was standing by the road-when he came by on horseback, and asked her to mount up behind him, and go riding. When she would not he vanished. The other was out on the road late at night waiting for her young man, when something came flapping and rolling along the road up to her feet. It had the likeness of a newspaper, and presently it flapped up into her face, and she knew by the size of it that it was the *Irish Times*. All of a sudden it changed into a young man, who asked her to go walking with him. She would not, and he vanished.

I know of an old man too, on the slopes of Ben Bulben, who found the Devil ringing a bell under his bed, and he went off and stole the chapel bell and rang him out.

The devil

HAPPY AND UNHAPPY THEOLOGIANS

I

A MAYO woman once said to me, 'I knew a servant-girl who hung herself for the love of God. She was lonely for the priest and her society,* and hung herself to the banisters with a scarf. She was no sooner dead than she became white as a lily, and if it had been murder or suicide she would have become black as black. They gave her Christian burial, and the priest said she was no sooner dead than she was with the Lord. So nothing matters that you do for the love of God.' I do not wonder at the pleasure she has in telling this story, for she herself loves all holy things with an ardour that brings them quickly to her lips. She told me once that she never hears anything described in a sermon that she does not afterwards see with her eyes. She has described to me the gates of Purgatory as they showed themselves to her eyes, but I remember nothing of the description except that she could not see the souls in trouble but only the gates. Her mind continually dwells on what is pleasant and beautiful. One day she asked me what month and what flower were the most beautiful. When I answered that I did not know, she said 'The month of May, because of the Virgin, and the lily of the valley, because it never sinned, but came pure out of the rocks,' and then she asked, 'What is the cause of the three cold months of winter?' I did not know even that, and so she said, 'The sin of man and the vengeance of God.' Christ Himself was not only blessed, but perfect in all manly proportions in her eyes, so much do beauty and holiness go together in her thoughts. He alone of all men was exactly six

* The religious society she had belonged to.

feet high, all others are a little more or a little less.

Her thoughts and her sights of the people of Faery are pleasant and beautiful too, and I have never heard her call them the Fallen Angels. They are people like ourselves, only better-looking, and many and many a time she has gone to the window to watch them drive their wagons through the sky, wagon behind wagon in long line, or to the door to hear them singing and dancing in the forth. They sing chiefly, it seems, a song called 'The Distant Waterfall', and though they once knocked her down she never thinks badly of them. She saw them most easily when she was in service in King's County, and one morning a little while ago she said to me, 'Last night I was waiting up for the master and it was a quarter-past eleven. I heard a bang right down on the table. "King's County all over," says I, and I laughed till I was near dead. It was a warning I was staying too long. They wanted the place to themselves.' I told her once of somebody who saw a faery and fainted, and she said, 'It could not have been a faery but some bad thing, nobody could faint at a faery. It was a demon. I was not afraid when they near put me, and the bed under me, out through the roof. I wasn't afraid either when you were at some work and I heard a thing coming flop-flop up the stairs like an eel, and squealing. It went to all the doors. It could not get in where I was. I would have sent it through the universe like a flash of fire. There was a man in my place, a tearing fellow, and he put one of them down. He went out to meet it on the road, but he must have been told the words. But the faeries are the best neighbours. If you do good to them they will do good to you, but they don't like you to be on their path.' Another time she said to me, 'They are always good to the poor.'

II

There is, however, a man in a Galway village who can see nothing but wickedness. Some think him very holy, and others think him a little crazed, but some of his talk reminds one of those old Irish visions of the Three Worlds, which are supposed to have given Dante the plan of the *Divine Comedy*. But I could not imagine this man seeing Paradise. He is especially angry with the people of Faery, and describes the faun-like feet that are so common among them, who are indeed children of Pan, to prove them children of Satan. He will not grant that 'they carry away women, though there are many that say so,' but he is certain that they are 'as thick as the sands of the sea about us, and they tempt poor mortals.'

He says, 'There is a priest I know of was looking along the ground like as if he was hunting for something, and a voice said to him, "If you want to see them you'll see enough of them," and his eyes were opened and he saw the ground thick with them. Singing they do be sometimes, and dancing, but all the time they have cloven feet,' Yet he was so scornful of unchristian beings for all their dancing and singing that he thinks that 'you have only to bid them begone and they will go. It was one night,' he says, 'after walking back from Kinvara and down by the wood beyond I felt one coming beside me, and I could feel the horse he was riding on and the way he lifted his legs, but they do not make a sound like the hoofs of a horse. So I stopped and turned around and said, very loud, "Be off!" and he went and never troubled me after. And I knew a man who was dying, and one came on his bed, and he cried out to it, "Get out of that, you unnatural animal!" and it left him. Fallen angels they are, and after the fall God said, "Let there be Hell," and there it was in a moment.' An old woman who was sitting by the fire joined in as he said this with 'God save us, it's a pity He said the word, and there might have been no Hell the day,' but the seer did not notice her words. He went on, 'And then he asked the Devil what would he take for the souls of all the people. And the Devil said nothing would satisfy him but the blood of a virgin's son, so he got that, and then the gates of Hell were opened.' He understood the story, it seems, as if it were some riddling old folk tale.

'I have seen Hell myself. I had a sight of it one time in a vision. It had a very high wall around it, all of metal, and an archway, and a straight walk into it, just like what 'ud be leading into a gentleman's orchard, but the edges were not trimmed with box, but with red-hot metal. And inside the wall there were cross-walks, and I'm not sure what there was to the right, but to the left there were five great furnaces, and they full of souls kept there with great chains. So I turned short and went away, and in turning I looked again at the wall, and I could see no end to it.

'And another time I saw Purgatory. It seemed to be in a level place, and no walls around it, but it all one bright blaze, and the souls standing in it. And they suffer near as much as in Hell, only there are no devils with them there, and they have the hope of Heaven.

'And I heard a call to me from there, "Help me to come out o' this!" And when I looked it was a man I used to know in the Army, an Irishman, and from this county, and I believe him to be a descendant of King O'Connor of Athenry.

'So I stretched out my hand first, but then I called out, "I'd be burned in the flames before I could get within three yards of you." So then he said, "Well, help me with your prayers," and so I do.

'And Father Connellan says the same thing, to help the dead with your prayers, and he's a very clever man to make a sermon, and has a great deal of cures made with the Holy Water he brought back from Lourdes.'

1902.

THE LAST GLEEMAN

MICHAEL MORAN was born about 1794 off Black Pitts, in the Liberties of Dublin, in Faddle Alley. A fortnight after birth he went stone blind from illness, and became thereby a blessing to his parents, who were soon able to send him to rhyme and beg at street corners and at the bridges over the Liffey. They may well have wished that their quiver were full of such as he, for, free from the interruption of sight, his mind turned every movement of the day and every change of public passion into rhyme or quaint saying. By the time he had grown to manhood he was the admitted rector of all the balladmongers of the Liberties, of Madden, the weaver, Kearney, the blind fiddler from Wicklow, Martin from Meath, M'Bride from Heaven knows where, and that M'Grane, who in after days, when the true Moran was no more, strutted in borrowed plumes, or rather in borrowed rags, and gave out that there had never been any Moran but himself, and many another. Nor despite his blindness did he find any difficulty in getting a wife, but rather was able to pick and choose, for he was just that mixture of ragamuffin and of genius which is dear to the heart of woman, who, however conventional in herself, loves the unexpected, the crooked, the bewildering. Nor did he lack, despite his rags, many excellent things, for it is remembered that he ever loved caper sauce, and upon one occasion when his wife had forgotten it, he flung a leg of mutton at her head. He was not, certainly, much to look at, with his coarse frieze coat with its cape and scalloped edge, his old corduroy trousers and great brogues, and his stout stick made fast to his wrist by a thong of leather: and he would have been a woeful shock to the gleeman MacCoinglinne, could that friend of kings have beheld him in prophetic vision from the pillar stone at Cork. And yet though the short cloak and the leather wallet were no more, he was a true gleeman, being alike poet, jester, and newsman of the people. In the morning when he had finished his breakfast, his wife or some neighbour would read the newspaper to him, and read on and on until he interrupted with, 'That'll do—I have me meditations'; and from these meditations would come the day's store of jest and rhyme. He had the whole Middle Ages under his frieze coat.

He had not, however, MacCoinglinne's hatred of the Church and clergy, for when the fruit of his meditations did not ripen well, or when the crowd called for something more solid, he would recite or sing a metrical tale or ballad of saint or martyr or some Biblical adventure. He would stand at a street corner, and when a crowd had gathered would begin in some such fashion as follows (I copy the record of one who knew him):— 'Gather round me, boys, gather round me. Boys, am I standin' in puddle? am I standin' in wet?' Thereon several boys would cry, 'Ah, no! yez not! yer in a nice dry place. Go on with *Saint Mary*; go on with *Moses*'—each calling for his favourite tale. Then Moran, with a wriggle of his body and a clutch at his rags, would burst out with, 'All me buzzim friends are turned backbiters'; and after a final warning to the boys, 'If yez don't drop your coddin' and diversion I'll lave some of yez a case,' begin his recitation, or perhaps still delay, to ask, 'Is there a crowd round me now? Any blaguard heretic around me?' Or he would, it may be, start by singing:—

> Gather round me, boys, will yez
> Gather round me?
> And hear what I have to say
> Before ould Sally brings me
> My bread and jug of tay.

The best-known of his religious tales was *Saint Mary of Egypt*,

a long poem of exceeding solemnity, condensed from the
much longer work of a certain Bishop Coyle. It told how an
Egyptian harlot, Mary by name, followed pilgrims to Jeru-
salem in pursuit of her trade, and then, on finding herself
withheld from entering the Temple by supernatural inter-
ference, turned penitent, fled to the desert and spent the
remainder of her life in solitary penance. When at last she was
at the point of death, God sent Bishop Zosimus to hear her
confession, give her the last sacrament, and with the help of
a lion, whom He sent also, dig her grave. The poem has the
intolerable cadence of the eighteenth century at its worst,
but was so popular and so often called for that Moran was
nicknamed Zosimus, and by that name is he remembered.
He had also a poem of his own called *Moses*, which went a
little nearer poetry without going very near. But he could
ill brook solemnity, and before long parodied his own verses
in the following ragamuffin fashion:—

> In Egypt's land, contagious to the Nile,
> King Pharaoh's daughter went to bathe in style.
> She tuk her dip, then walked unto the land,
> To dry her royal pelt she ran along the strand.
> A bulrush tripped her, whereupon she saw
> A smiling babby in a wad o' straw.
> She tuk it up, and said with accents mild,
> ''Tare-and-agers, girls, which av yez owns the child?'

His humorous rhymes were, however, more often quips and
cranks at the expense of his contemporaries. It was his
delight, for instance, to remind a shoemaker, noted alike for
display of wealth and for personal uncleanness, of his incon-
siderable origin in a song of which but the first stanza has
come down to us:—

> At the dirty end of Dirty Lane,
> Liv'd a dirty cobbler, Dick Maclane;
> His wife was in the old King's reign
> A stout brave orange-woman.

73

On Essex Bridge she strained her throat,
And six-a-penny was her note.
But Dickey wore a bran-new coat
  He got among the yeomen.
He was a bigot, like his clan,
And in the streets he wildly sang,
  O Roly, toly, toly raid, with his old jade.

He had troubles of divers kinds, and numerous interlopers to face and put down. Once an officious peeler arrested him as a vagabond, but was triumphantly routed amid the laughter of the court, when Moran reminded his worship of the precedent set by Homer, who was also, he declared, a poet, and a blind man, and a beggar-man. He had to face a more serious difficulty as his fame grew. Various imitators started up upon all sides. A certain actor, for instance, made as many guineas as Moran did shillings by mimicking his sayings and his songs and his get-up upon the stage. One night this actor was at supper with some friends, when dispute arose as to whether his mimicry was overdone or not. It was agreed to settle it by an appeal to the mob. A forty-shilling supper at a famous coffee-house was to be the wager. The actor took up his station at Essex Bridge, a great haunt of Moran's, and soon gathered a small crowd. He had scarce got through 'In Egypt's land, contagious to the Nile,' when Moran himself came up, followed by another crowd. The crowds met in great excitement and laughter. 'Good Christians,' cried the pretender, 'is it possible that any man would mock the poor dark man like that?'

'Who's that? It's some imposhterer,' replied Moran.

'Begone, you wretch! it's you'se the imposhterer. Don't you fear the light of heaven being struck from your eyes for mocking the poor dark man?'

'Saints and angels, is there no protection against this? You're a most inhuman blaguard to try to deprive me of my honest bread this way,' replied the poor Moran.

'And you, you wretch, won't let me go on with the beautiful poem? Christian people, in your charity won't you beat this man away? he's taking advantage of my darkness.'

The pretender, seeing that he was having the best of it, thanked the people for their sympathy and protection, and went on with the poem, Moran listening for a time in bewildered silence. After a while Moran protested again with:—

'Is it possible that none of yez can know me? Don't yez see it's myself; and that's some one else?'

'Before I can proceed any further in this lovely story,' interrupted the pretender, 'I call on yez to contribute your charitable donations to help me to go on.'

'Have you no sowl to be saved, you mocker of Heaven?' cried Moran, put completely beside himself by this last injury. 'Would you rob the poor as well as desave the world? O, was ever such wickedness known?'

'I leave it to yourselves, my friends,' said the pretender, 'to give to the real dark man, that you all know so well, and save me from that schemer,' and with that he collected some pennies and halfpence. While he was doing so, Moran started his *Mary of Egypt*, but the indignant crowd seizing his stick were about to belabour him, when they fell back bewildered anew by his close resemblance to himself. The pretender now called to them to 'just give him a grip of that villain, and he'd soon let him know who the imposhterer was!' They led him over to Moran, but instead of closing with him he thrust a few shillings into his hand, and turning to the crowd explained to them he was indeed but an actor, and that he had just gained a wager, and so departed amid much enthusiasm, to eat the supper he had won.

In April 1846 word was sent to the priest that Michael Moran was dying. He found him at 15 (now 14½) Patrick Street, on a straw bed, in a room full of ragged ballad-singers come to cheer his last moments. After his death the ballad-singers, with many fiddles and the like, came again and gave him a fine wake, each adding to the merriment whatever he knew in the way of rann, tale, old saw, or quaint rhyme. He had had his day, had said his prayers and made his confession, and why should they not give him a hearty send-off? The funeral took place the next day. A good party of his admirers and friends got into the hearse with the coffin, for the day was wet and nasty. They had not gone far when one of them burst out with, 'It's cruel cowld, isn't it?' 'Garra',' replied another, 'we'll all be as stiff as the corpse when we get to the berrin'-ground.' 'Bad cess to him,' said a third; 'I wish he'd held out another month until the weather got dacent.' A man called Carroll thereupon produced a half-pint of whiskey, and they all drank to the soul of the departed. Unhappily, however, the hearse was over-weighted, and they had not reached the cemetery before the spring broke, and the bottle with it.

REGINA, REGINA PIGMEORUM, VENI*

ONE night a middle-aged man, who had lived all his life far from the noise of cab-wheels, a young girl, a relation of his, who was reported to be enough of a seeress to catch a glimpse of unaccountable lights moving over the fields among the cattle, and myself, were walking along a far western sandy shore. We talked of the Forgetful People, as the faery people are sometimes called, and came in the midst of our talk to a notable haunt of theirs, a shallow cave amidst black rocks, with its reflection under it in the wet sea sand. I asked the young girl if she could see anything, for I had quite a number of things to ask the Forgetful People. She stood still for a few minutes, and I saw that she was passing into a kind of waking trance, in which the cold sea breeze no longer troubled her, nor the dull boom of the sea distracted her attention. I then called aloud the names of the great faeries, and in a moment or two she said that she could hear music far inside the rocks, and then a sound of confused talking, and of people stamping their feet as if to applaud some unseen performer. Up to this my other friend had been walking to and fro some yards off, but now he passed close to us, and as he did so said suddenly that we were going to be interrupted, for he heard the laughter of children somewhere beyond the rocks. We were, however, quite alone. The spirits of the place had begun to cast their influence over him also. In a moment he was corroborated by the girl, who said that bursts of laughter had begun to

* These words were used as an evocation in Windsor Forest by Lilly, the astrologer. (1924.)

77

The queen of the little people

mingle with the music, the confused talking, and the noise of feet. She next saw a bright light streaming out of the cave, which seemed to have grown much deeper, and a quantity of little people,* in various coloured dresses. red predominating, dancing to a tune which she did not recognise.

I then bade her call out to the queen of the little people to come and talk with us. There was, however, no answer to her command. I therefore repeated the words aloud myself, and in a moment she described a very beautiful tall woman, who came out of the cave. I too had by this time fallen into a kind of trance,† in which what we call the unreal had begun to take upon itself a masterful reality, and I had an impression, not anything I could call an actual vision, of gold ornaments and dark hair. I then bade the girl tell this tall queen to marshal her followers according to their natural divisions, that we might see them. I found as before that I had to repeat the command myself. The beings then came out of the cave, and drew themselves up, if I remember rightly, in four bands. One of these bands, according to her description, carried boughs of mountain-ash in their hands, and another had necklaces made apparently of serpents' scales, but their dress I cannot remember. I asked their queen to tell the seeress whether these caves were the greatest faery haunts in the neighbourhood. Her lips moved, but the answer was inaudible. I bade the seeress lay her hand upon the breast of the queen, and after that she heard every word quite distinctly. No, this was not the greatest faery haunt, for there

* The people and faeries in Ireland are sometimes as big as we are, sometimes bigger, and sometimes, as I have been told, about three feet high. The old Mayo woman I so often quote thinks that it is something in our eyes that makes them seem big or little.
† The word 'trance' gives a wrong impression. I had learned from Mac-Gregor Mathers and his pupils to so suspend the will that the imagination moved of itself. The girl was, however, fully entranced, and the man so affected by her that he heard the children's voices as if with his physical ears. On two occasions, later on, her trance so affected me that I also heard or saw some part of what she did as if with physical eyes and ears. (1924.)

was a greater one a little farther ahead. I then asked her whether it was true that she and her people carried away mortals, and if so, whether they put another soul in the place of the one they had taken. 'We change the bodies,' was her answer. 'Are any of you ever born into mortal life?' 'Yes.' 'Do I know any who were among your people before birth?' 'You do.' 'Who are they?' 'It would not be lawful for you to know.' I then asked whether she and her people were not 'dramatisations of our moods?' 'She does not understand,' said my friend, 'but says that her people are much like human beings, and do most of the things human beings do.' I asked her other questions, as to her nature, and her purpose in the universe, but only seemed to puzzle her. At last she appeared to lose patience, for she wrote this message for me upon the sands—the sands of vision—'Be careful, and do not seek to know too much about us.' Seeing that I had offended her, I thanked her for what she had shown and told, and let her depart again into her cave. In a little while the young girl awoke out of her trance, and felt the cold wind from the sea, and began to shiver.

'AND FAIR, FIERCE WOMEN'

ONE DAY a woman that I know came face to face with heroic beauty, that highest beauty which Blake says changes least from youth to age, a beauty which has been fading out of the arts, since that decadence we call progress set voluptuous beauty in its place. She was standing at the window, looking over to Knocknarea where Queen Maeve is thought to be buried, when she saw, as she has told me, 'the finest woman you ever saw, travelling right across from the mountains and straight to her.' The woman had a sword by her side and a dagger lifted up in her hand, and was dressed in white, with bare arms and feet. She looked 'very strong, but not wicked,' that is, not cruel. The old woman had seen the Irish giant, and 'though he was a fine man,' he was nothing to this woman, 'for he was round, and could not have stepped out so soldierly'; 'she was like Mrs. ——' (a stately lady of the neighbourhood) 'but she had no stomach on her, and was slight and broad in the shoulders, and was handsomer than any one you ever saw; she looked about thirty.' The old woman covered her eyes with her hands, and when she uncovered them the apparition had vanished. The neighbours were 'wild with her,' she told me, because she did not wait to find out if there was a message, for they were sure it was Queen Maeve, who often shows herself to the pilots. I asked the old woman if she had seen others like Queen Maeve, and she said, 'Some of them have their hair down, but they look quite different, like the sleepy-looking ladies one sees in the papers. Those with their hair up are like this one. The others have long white dresses, but those with their hair up have short dresses, so that you can see their legs right up to the calf.' After some careful questioning I found that they wore what might very well be a kind of buskin; she went on, 'They are fine and dashing looking, like the men one sees riding their horses in twos and threes on the slopes of the mountains with their swords swinging.' She repeated over and over, 'There is no race living now, none so finely proportioned,' or the like, and then said, 'The present Queen* is a nice, pleasant-looking woman, but she is not like her. What makes me think so little of the ladies is that I see none as they be,' meaning as the spirits. 'When I think of her and of the ladies now, they are like little children running about without knowing how to put their clothes on right. Is it the ladies? Why, I would not call them women at all.' The other day a friend of mine questioned an old woman in a Galway workhouse about Queen Maeve, and was told that 'Queen Maeve was handsome, and overcame all her enemies with a hazel stick, for the hazel is blessed, and the best weapon that can be got. You might walk the world with it,' but she grew 'very disagreeable in the end—O very disagreeable. Best not to be talking about it. Best leave it between the book and the hearer.' My friend thought the old woman had got some scandal about Fergus son of Rogh and Maeve in her head.

And I myself met once with a young man in the Burren Hills who remembered an old poet who made his poems in Irish and had met when he was young, the young man said, one who called herself Maeve, and said she was a queen 'among them', and asked him if he would money or pleasure. He said he would have pleasure, and she gave him her love for a time, and then went from him, and ever after he was very mournful. The young man had often heard him sing the poem of lamentation that he made, but could only remember that it was 'very mournful', and that he called her 'beauty of all beauties.'

1902.

* Queen Victoria.

82

ENCHANTED WOODS

I

LAST SUMMER, whenever I had finished my day's work, I used to go wandering in certain roomy woods, and there I would often meet an old countryman, and talk to him about his work and about the woods, and once or twice a friend came with me to whom he would open his heart more readily than to me. He had spent all his life lopping away the witch-elm and the hazel and the privet and the hornbeam from the paths, and had thought much about the natural and supernatural creatures of the wood. He has heard the hedgehog—'grainne oge,' he calls him—'grunting like a Christian,' and is certain that he steals apples by rolling about under an apple-tree until there is an apple sticking to every quill. He is certain too that the cats, of whom there are many in the woods, have a language of their own—some kind of old Irish. He says, Cats were serpents, and they were made into cats at the time of some great change in the world. That is why they are hard to kill, and why it is dangerous to meddle with them. If you annoy a cat it might claw or bite you in a way that would put poison in you, and that would be the serpent's tooth.' Sometimes he thinks they change into wild cats, and then a nail grows on the end of their tails: but these wild cats are not the same as the marten cats, who have been always in the woods. The foxes were once tame, as the cats are now, but they ran away and became wild. He talks of all wild creatures except squirrels—whom he hates—with what seems an affectionate interest, though at times his eyes will twinkle with pleasure as he remembers how he made hedgehogs unroll themselves when he was a boy, by putting a wisp of burning straw under them.

I am not certain that he distinguishes between the natural and supernatural very clearly. He told me the other day that foxes and cats like, above all, to be in the 'forths' and lisses after nightfall; and he will certainly pass from some story about a fox to a story about a spirit with less change of voice than when he is going to speak about a marten cat—a rare beast nowadays. Many years ago he used to work in the garden, and once they put him to sleep in a garden-house where there was a loft full of apples, and all night he could hear people rattling plates and knives and forks over his head in the loft. Once, at any rate, he has seen an unearthly sight in the woods. He says, 'One time I was out cutting timber over in Inchy, and about eight o'clock one morning when I got there I saw a girl picking nuts, with her hair hanging down over her shoulders, brown hair, and she had a good, clean face, and she was tall and nothing on her head, and her dress no way gaudy but simple, and when she felt me coming she gathered herself up and was gone as if the earth had swallowed her up. And I followed her and looked for her, but I never could see her again from that day to this, never again.' He used the word clean as we would use words like fresh or comely.

Others too have seen spirits in the Enchanted Woods. A labourer told us of what a friend of his had seen in a part of the woods that is called Shan-walla, from some old village that was before the wood. He said, 'One evening I parted from Lawrence Mangan in the yard, an' he went away through the path in Shan-walla, an' bid me good-night. And two hours after, there he was back again in the yard, an' bid me light a candle that was in the stable. An' he told me that when he got into Shan-walla, a little fellow about as high as his knee, but having a head as big as a man's body, came beside him and led him out of the path an' round about, and at last it brought him to the lime-kiln, and then it vanished and left him.'

A woman told me of a sight that she and others had seen by a certain deep pool in the river. She said, 'I came over the stile from the chapel, and others along with me; and a great blast of wind came and two trees were bent and broken and fell into the river, and the splash of water out of it went up to the skies. And those that were with me saw many figures, but myself I only saw one, sitting there by the bank where the trees fell. Dark clothes he had on, and he was headless.'

A man told me that one day, when he was a boy, he and another boy went to catch a horse in a certain field, full of boulders and bushes of hazel and creeping juniper and rock-roses, that is where the lake-side is for a little clear of the woods. He said to the boy that was with him, 'I bet a button that if I fling a pebble on to that bush it will stay on it,' meaning that the bush was so matted the pebble would not be able to go through it. So he took up 'a pebble of cow-dung, and as soon as it hit the bush there came out of it the most beautiful music that ever was heard.' They ran away, and when they had gone about two hundred yards they looked back and saw a woman dressed in white, walking round and round the bush. 'First it had the form of a woman, and then of a man, and it was going round the bush.'

II

I often entangle myself in arguments more complicated than even those paths of Inchy as to what is the true nature of apparitions. But at other times I say as Socrates said when they told him a learned opinion about a nymph of the Ilissus, 'The common opinion is enough for me'; and believe that all nature is full of invisible people, and that some of these are ugly or grotesque, some wicked or foolish, many beautiful beyond any one we have ever seen, and that the beautiful are not far away when we are walking in pleasant and quiet places. Even when I was a boy I could never walk in a wood without feeling that at any moment I might find before me somebody or something I had long looked for without knowing what I looked for. And now I will at times explore every little nook of some poor coppice with almost anxious footsteps, so deep a hold has this imagination upon me. You too meet with a like imagination, doubtless, somewhere, wherever your ruling stars will have it, Saturn driving you to the woods, or the Moon, it may be, to the edges of the sea. I will not of a certainty believe that there is nothing in the sunset, where our forefathers imagined the dead following their shepherd the sun, or nothing but some vague presence as little moving as nothing. If beauty is not a gateway out of the net we were taken in at our birth, it will not long be beauty, and we will find it better to sit at home by the fire and fatten a lazy body or to run hither and thither in some foolish sport than to look at the finest show that light and shadow ever made among green leaves. I say to myself, when I am well out of that thicket of argument, that they are surely there, the divine people, for only we who have neither simplicity nor wisdom have denied them, and the simple of all times and the wise men of ancient times have seen them and even spoken to them. They live out their passionate lives not far off, as I think, and we shall be among them when we die if we but keep our natures simple and passionate. May it not even be that death shall unite us to all romance, and that some day we shall fight dragons among blue hills, or come to that whereof all romance is but

> Foreshadowings mingled with the images
> Of man's misdeeds in greater days than these,

as the old men thought in *The Earthly Paradise* when they were in good spirits?

1902.

MIRACULOUS CREATURES

THERE ARE marten cats and badgers and foxes in the Enchanted Woods, but there are, it seems, mightier creatures, and the lake may hide what neither net or line can take. These creatures are of the race of the white stag that flits in and out of the tales of Arthur, and of the evil pig that slew Diarmuid where Ben Bulben mixes with the sea wind. They are, as I conceive it, the wizard creatures of hope and fear, they are of them that fly and of them that follow among the thickets that are about the Gates of Death. A man I know remembers that his father was one night in the wood of Inchy, 'where the lads of Gort used to be stealing rods. He was sitting by the wall, and the dog beside him, and he heard something come running from Owbarn Weir, and he could see nothing, but the sound of its feet on the ground was like the sound of the feet of a deer. And when it passed him, the dog got between him and the wall and scratched at it there as if it was afraid, but still he could see nothing but only hear the sound of hoofs. So when it was past he turned and came away home.' 'Another time,' the man says, 'my father told me he was in a boat out on the lake with two or three men from Gort, and one of them had an eel-spear, and he thrust it into the water, and it hit something, and the man fainted and they had to carry him out of the boat to land, and when he came to himself he said that what he struck was like a calf, but whatever it was, it was not fish!'

1902.

87

ARISTOTLE OF THE BOOKS

THE FRIEND who can get the wood-cutter to talk more readily than he will to anybody else went lately to see his old wife. She lives in a cottage not far from the edge of the woods, and is as full of old talk as her husband. This time she began to talk of Goban, the legendary mason, and his wisdom, but said presently, 'Aristotle of the Books, too, was very wise, and he had a great deal of experience, but did not the bees get the better of him in the end? He wanted to know how they packed the comb, and he wasted the better part of a fortnight watching them, and he could not see them doing it. Then he made a hive with a glass cover on it and put it over them, and he thought to see. But when he went and put his eyes to the glass, they had it all covered with wax so that it was as black as the pot; and he was as blind as before. He said he was never rightly kilt till then. They had him that time surely!'

1902.

THE SWINE OF THE GODS

A FEW YEARS ago a friend of mine told me of something that happened to him when he was a young
man and out drilling with some Connacht Fenians.
They were but a carful, and drove along a hillside until they
came to a quiet place. They left the car and went farther up
the hill with their rifles, and drilled for a while. As they were
coming down again they saw a very thin, long-legged pig of
the old Irish sort, and the pig began to follow them. One of
them cried out as a joke that it was a faery pig, and they all
began to run to keep up the joke. The pig ran too, and
presently, how nobody knew, this mock terror became real
terror, and they ran as for their lives. When they got to the
car they made the horse gallop as fast as possible, but the pig
still followed. Then one of them put up his rifle to fire, but
when he looked along the barrel he could see nothing.
Presently they turned a corner and came to a village. They
told the people of the village what had happened, and the
people of the village took pitchforks and spades and the like,
and went along the road with them to drive the pig away.
When they turned the corner they could not find anything.

1902.

A VOICE

ONE DAY I was walking over a bit of marshy ground close to Inchy Wood when I felt, all of a sudden, and only for a second, an emotion which I said to myself was the root of Christian mysticism. There had swept over me a sense of weakness, of dependence on a great personal Being somewhere far off yet near at hand. No thought of mine had prepared me for this emotion, for I had been preoccupied with Aengus and Edain, and with Manannan, Son of the Sea. That night I awoke lying upon my back and hearing a voice speaking above me and saying, 'No human soul is like any other human soul, and therefore the love of God for any human soul is infinite, for no other soul can satisfy the same need in God.' A few nights after this I awoke to see the loveliest people I have ever seen. A young man and a young girl dressed in olive-green raiment, cut like old Greek raiment, were standing at my bedside. I looked at the girl and noticed that her dress was gathered about her neck into a kind of chain, or perhaps into some kind of stiff embroidery which represented ivy-leaves. But what filled me with wonder was the miraculous mildness of her face. There are no such faces now. It was beautiful as few faces are beautiful, but it had not, one would think, the light that is in desire or in hope or in fear or in speculation. It was peaceful like the faces of animals, or like mountain pools at evening, so peaceful that it was a little sad. I thought for a moment that she might be the beloved of Aengus, but how could that hunted, alluring, happy, immortal wretch have a face like this?

1902.

90

KIDNAPPERS

A LITTLE NORTH of the town of Sligo, on the southern side of Ben Bulben, some hundreds of feet above the plain, is a small white square in the limestone. No mortal has ever touched it with his hand; no sheep or goat has ever browsed grass behind it. There is no more inaccessible place upon the earth, and to an anxious consideration few more encircled by terror. It is the door of Faeryland. In the middle of night it swings open, and the unearthly troop rushes out. All night the gay rabble sweep to and fro across the land, invisible to all, unless perhaps where, in some more than commonly 'gentle' place—Drumcliff or Dromahair, the night-capped heads of 'faery-doctors' or 'cow-doctors' may be thrust from their doors to see what mischief the 'gentry' are doing. To their trained eyes and ears doubtless the fields are covered by red-hatted riders, and the air is full of shrill voices—a sound like whistling, as an ancient Scottish seer has recorded, and wholly different from the talk of the angels, who 'speak much in the throat, like the Irish,' as Lilly, the astrologer, has wisely said. If there be a new-born baby or new-wed bride in the neighbourhood, the 'doctors' will peer with more than common care, for the unearthly troop do not always return empty-handed. Sometimes a new-wed bride or a new-born baby goes with them into their mountains; the door swings to behind, and the new-born or the new-wed moves henceforth in the bloodless land of Faery; happy, the story has it, but doomed to melt at the Last Judgement like bright vapour, for the soul cannot live without sorrow. Through this door of white stone, and the other doors of that land where *geabhadh tu an sonas aer phingin* ('you can buy joy for a penny'), have gone those kings, queens, and princes whose stories are in our old Gaelic literature.

There suddenly appeared at the western corner of Market Street, Sligo, where the butcher's shop now is, as did a palace in Keats's *Lamia*, an apothecary's shop, ruled over by a certain unaccountable Dr. Opendon. Where he came from, none ever knew. There also was in Sligo, in those days, a woman, Ormsby by name, whose husband had fallen mysteriously sick. The doctors could make nothing of him. Nothing seemed wrong with him, yet weaker and weaker he grew. Away went the wife to Dr. Opendon. She was shown into the shop parlour. A black cat was sitting straight up before the fire. She had just time to see that the sideboard was covered with fruit, and to say to herself, 'Fruit must be wholesome when the doctor has so much,' before Dr. Opendon came in. He was dressed all in black, the same as the cat, and his wife walked behind him dressed in black likewise. She gave him a guinea, and got a little bottle in return. Her husband recovered that time. Meanwhile, the black doctor cured many people; but one day a rich patient died, and cat, wife, and doctor all vanished the night after. In a year the man Ormsby fell sick once more. Now he was a good-looking man, and his wife felt sure the 'gentry' were coveting him. She went and called on the 'faery-doctor' at Cairnsfoot. As soon as he had heard her tale, he went behind the back door and began muttering spells. Her husband got well this time also. But after a while he sickened again, the fatal third time, and away went she once more to Cairnsfoot, and out went the 'faery-doctor' behind his back door and began muttering, but soon he came in and told her it was no use—her husband would die; and sure enough the man died, and ever after when she spoke of him Mrs. Ormsby shook her head saying she knew well where he was, and it wasn't in Heaven or Hell or Purgatory either. She probably believed that a log of wood was left behind in his place, but so bewitched that it seemed the dead body of her husband.

She is dead now herself, but many still living remember

her. She was, I believe, for a time a servant or else a kind of pensioner of some relations of my own.

Sometimes those who are carried off are allowed after many years—seven usually—a final glimpse of their friends. Many years ago a woman vanished suddenly from a Sligo garden where she was walking with her husband. When her son, who was then a baby, had grown up he received word in some way, not handed down, that his mother was glamoured by faeries, and imprisoned for the time in a house in Glasgow and longing to see him. Glasgow in those days of sailing ships seemed to the peasant mind almost over the edge of the known world, yet he, being a dutiful son, started away. For a long time he walked the streets of Glasgow; at last down in a cellar he saw his mother working. She was happy, she said, and had the best of good eating, and would he not eat? and therewith laid all kinds of food on the table; but, he knowing well that she was trying to cast on him the glamour by giving him faery food, that she might keep him with her, refused and came home to his people in Sligo.

Some five miles southward of Sligo is a gloomy and tree-bordered pond, a great gathering place of water-fowl, called, because of its form, the Heart Lake. Out of this lake, as from the white square stone in Ben Bulben, issues an unearthly troop. Once men began to drain it; suddenly one of them raised a cry that he saw his house in flames. They turned round, and every man there saw his own house burning. They hurried home to find it was but faery glamour. To this hour on the border of the lake is shown a half-dug trench—the signet of their impiety. A little way from this lake I heard a beautiful and mournful history of faery kidnapping. I heard it from a little old woman in a white cap, who sings in Gaelic, and moves from one foot to the other as though she remembered the dancing of her youth.

A young man going at nightfall to the house of his just-married bride, met on the way a jolly company, and with them his bride. They were faeries and had stolen her as a wife for the chief of their band. To him they seemed only a company of merry mortals. His bride, when she saw her old

The tale of the bride stolen by the faeries

love bade him welcome, but was most fearful lest he should eat the faery food, and so be glamoured out of the earth into that bloodless dim nation, wherefore she set him down to play cards with three of the cavalcade; and he played on, realising nothing until he saw the chief of the band carrying his bride away in his arms. Immediately he started up, and knew that they were faeries, for all that jolly company melted into shadow and night. He hurried to his house, and as he drew near heard the cry of the keeners and knew that his wife was dead. Some noteless Gaelic poet had made this into a forgotten ballad, some odd verses of which my white-capped friend remembers and sang for me.*

Sometimes one hears of stolen people acting as good genii to the living, as in this tale, heard also close by the haunted pond, of John Kirwan of Castle Hackett. The Kirwans† are a family much rumoured of in peasant stories, and believed to be the descendants of a man and a spirit. They have ever been famous for beauty, and I have read that the mother of the present Lord Cloncurry was of their tribe.

John Kirwan was a great horse-racing man, and once landed in Liverpool with a fine horse, going racing somewhere in middle England. That evening, as he walked by the docks, a slip of a boy came up and asked where he was stabling his horse. In such-and-such a place, he answered. 'Don't put him there,' said the slip of a boy; 'that stable will be burnt to-night.' He took his horse elsewhere, and sure enough the stable was burnt down. Next day the boy came and asked as reward to ride as his jockey in the coming race, and then was gone. The race-time came round. At the last moment the boy ran forward and mounted saying, 'If I strike him with the whip in my left hand I will lose, but if in my right bet all you are worth.' For, said Paddy Flynn, who told me the tale, 'the left arm is good for nothing. I might go on making the sign of the cross with

* There is a ballad in my *Wind among the Reeds* on this theme. (1924.)

† I have since heard that it was not the Kirwans, but their predecessors at Castle Hackett, the Hacketts themselves, I think, who were descended from a man and a spirit, and were notable for beauty. I imagine that the mother of Lord Cloncurry was descended from the Hacketts. It may well be that all through these stories the name of Kirwan has taken the place of the older name. (1902.) Castle Hackett was burned by incendiaries during our civil war. (1924.)

it, and all that, come Christmas, and a Banshee would no more mind than if it was that broom.' Well, the slip of a boy struck the horse with his right hand, and John Kirwan cleared the field out. When the race was over, 'What can I do for you now?' said he. 'Nothing but this,' said the boy: 'my mother has a cottage on your land—they stole me from the cradle. Be good to her, John Kirwan, and wherever your horses go I will watch that no ill follows them; but you will never see me more.' With that he made himself air, and vanished.

Sometimes animals are carried off—apparently drowned animals more than others. In Claremorris, Mayo, Paddy Flynn told me, lived a poor widow with one cow and its calf. The cow fell into the river and was washed away. There was a man thereabouts who went to a red-haired woman- for such are supposed to be wise in these things—and she told him to take the calf down to the edge of the river, and hide himself and watch. He did as she had told him, and as evening came on the calf began to low, and after a while the cow came along the edge of the river and commenced suckling it. Then, as he had been told, he caught the cow's tail. Away they went at a great pace, across hedges and ditches, till they came to a royalty—Paddy Flynn's name for a rath. Therein he saw walking or sitting all the people who had died out of his village in his time. A woman was sitting on the edge with a child on her knees, and she called out to him, to mind what the red-haired woman had told him, and he remembered she had said, 'Bleed the cow.' So he stuck his knife into the cow and drew blood. That broke the spell and he was able to turn her homeward. 'Do not forget the spancel,' said the woman with the child on her knees; 'take the inside one.' There were three spancels on a bush; he took one, and the cow was driven safely home to the widow.

There is hardly a valley or mountain-side where they cannot tell you of someone pillaged from amongst them. Two or three miles from the Heart Lake lives an old woman who was stolen away in her youth. After seven years she was brought home again for some reason or other, but she had no toes left. She had danced them off.

THE UNTIRING ONES

I T IS one of the great troubles of life that we cannot have
any unmixed emotions. There is always something in our
enemy that we like, and something in our sweetheart that
we dislike. It is this entanglement of moods which makes us
old, and puckers our brows and deepens the furrows about
our eyes. If we could love and hate with as good heart as the
Sidhe do, we might grow to be long-lived like them. But until
that day their untiring joys and sorrows must ever be one-half
of their fascination. Love with them never grows weary, nor
can the circles of the stars tire out their dancing feet. The
Donegal peasants remember this when they bend over the
spade, or sit full of the heaviness of the fields beside the
griddle at nightfall, and they tell stories about it that it may
not be forgotten. A short while ago, they say, two little
creatures, one like a young man, one like a young woman,
came to a farmer's house, and spent the night sweeping the
hearth and setting all tidy. The next night they came again,
and while the farmer was away, brought all the furniture
upstairs into one room, and having arranged it round the
walls, for the greater grandeur, it seems, they began to dance.
They danced on and on, and days and days went by, and all
the countryside came to look at them, but still their feet
never tired. The farmer did not dare to live at home the
while; and after three months he made up his mind to stand
it no more, and went and told them that the priest was
coming. The little creatures when they heard this went back
to their own country, and there their joy shall last as long as
the points of the rushes are brown, the people say, and this is

until God shall burn up the world with a kiss.

But it is not merely the Sidhe who know untiring days, for there have been men and women who, falling under their enchantment, have attained, perhaps by the right of their God-given spirits, an even more than faery abundance of life and feeling. Such a mortal was born long ago at a village in the south of Ireland. She lay asleep in a cradle, and her mother sat rocking her, when a woman of the Sidhe came in, and said that the child was chosen to be the bride of the prince of the dim kingdom, but that as it would never do for his wife to grow old and die while he was still in the first ardour of his love, she would be gifted with a faery life. The mother was to take the glowing log out of the fire and bury it in the garden, and her child would live as long as it remained unconsumed. The mother buried the log, and the child grew up, became a beauty, and married the prince, who came to her at nightfall. After seven hundred years the prince died, and another prince ruled in his stead and married the beautiful peasant girl in his turn; and after another seven hundred years he died also, and another prince and another husband came in his stead, and so on until she had had seven husbands. At last one day the priest of the parish called upon her, and told her that she was a scandal to the whole neighbourhood with her seven husbands and her long life. She was very sorry, she said, but she was not to blame, and then she told him about the log, and he went straight out and dug until he found it, and then they burned it, and she died, and was buried like a Christian, and everybody was pleased. Such a mortal too was Clooth-na-Bare,* who went all over the world seeking a lake deep enough to drown her faery life, of which she had grown weary, leaping from hill to lake and lake to hill, and setting up a cairn of stones wherever her feet

* Doubtless Clooth-na-Bare should be Cailleac Beare, which would mean the old Woman Beare. Beare or Bere or Verah or Dera or Dhera was a very famous person, perhaps the Mother of the Gods herself. Standish O'Grady found her, as he thinks, frequenting Lough Leath, or the Grey Lake on a mountain of the Fews. Perhaps Lough Ia is my mishearing, or the story-teller's mispronunciation of Lough Leath, for there are many Lough Leaths.

lighted, until at last she found the deepest water in the world in little Lough Ia, on the top of the Birds' Mountain at Sligo.

The two little creatures may well dance on, and the woman of the log and Clooth-na-Bare sleep in peace, for they have known untrammelled hate and unmixed love, and have never wearied themselves with 'yes' and 'no', or entangled their feet with the sorry net of 'maybe' and 'perhaps'. The great winds came and took them up into themselves.

EARTH, FIRE AND WATER

SOME FRENCH writer that I read when I was a boy said that the desert went into the heart of the Jews in their wanderings and made them what they are. I cannot remember by what argument he proved them to be even yet the indestructible children of earth, but it may well be that the elements have their children. If we knew the Fire-Worshippers better we might find that their centuries of pious observance have been rewarded, and that the fire has given them a little of its nature; and I am certain that the water, the water of the seas and of lakes and of mist and rain, has all but made the Irish after its image. Images form themselves in our minds perpetually as if they were reflected in some pool. We gave ourselves up in old times to mythology, and saw the gods everywhere. We talked to them face to face, and the stories of that communion are so many that I think they outnumber all the like stories of all the rest of Europe. Even to-day our countrypeople speak with the dead and with some who perhaps have never died as we understand death; and even our educated people pass without great difficulty into the condition of quiet that is the condition of vision. We can make our minds so like still water that beings gather about us that they may see, it may be, their own images, and so live for a moment with a clearer, perhaps even with a fiercer life because of our quiet. Did not the wise Porphyry think that all souls come to be born because of water, and that 'even the generation of images in the mind is from water'?

1902.

THE OLD TOWN

I FELL, ONE night some fifteen years ago into what seemed the power of Faery.

I had gone with a young man and his sister—friends and relations of my own—to pick stories out of an old countryman; and we were coming home talking over what he had told us. It was dark, and our imaginations were excited by his stories of apparitions, and this may have brought us, unknown to us, to the threshold, between sleeping and waking, where Sphinxes and Chimeras sit open-eyed and where there are always murmurings and whisperings. We had come under some trees that made the road very dark, when the girl saw a bright light moving slowly across the road. Her brother and myself saw nothing, and did not see anything until we had walked for about half an hour along the edge of the river and down a narrow lane to some fields where there were a ruined church covered with ivy, and the foundations of what was called 'the Old Town', which had been burned down, it was said, in Cromwell's day. We had stood for some few minutes, so far as I can recollect, looking over the fields full of stones and brambles and elder-bushes, when I saw a small bright light on the horizon, as it seemed, mounting up slowly towards the sky; then we saw other faint lights for a minute or two, and at last a bright flame like the flame of a torch moving rapidly over the river. We saw it all in such a dream, and it seems all so unreal, that I have never written of it until now, and hardly ever spoken of it, and even when thinking, because of some unreasonable impulse, I have avoided giving it weight in the argument. Perhaps I have felt that my recollections of things seen when the sense of reality was weakened must be untrustworthy. A few months ago, however, I talked it over with my two friends, and compared their somewhat meagre recollections with my own. That sense of unreality was all the more wonderful because the next day I heard sounds as unaccountable as were those lights, and without any emotion of unreality, and I remember them with perfect distinctness and confidence. The girl was sitting reading under a large old-fashioned mirror, and I was reading and writing a couple of yards away, when I heard a sound as if a shower of peas had been thrown against the mirror, and while I was looking at it I heard the sound again, and presently, while I was alone in the room, I heard a sound as if something much bigger than a pea had struck the wainscoting beside my head. And after that for some days came other sights and sounds, not to me but to the girl, her brother, and the servants. Now it was a bright light, now it was letters of fire that vanished before they could be read, now it was a heavy foot moving about in the seemingly empty house. One wonders whether creatures who live, the countrypeople believe, wherever men and women have lived in earlier times, followed us from the ruins of the old town? or did they come from the banks of the river by the trees where the first light had shone for a moment?

1902.

THE MAN AND HIS BOOTS

THERE was a doubter in Donegal, and he would not hear of ghosts or faeries, and there was a house in Donegal that had been haunted as long as man could remember, and this is the story of how the house got the better of the man. The man came into the house and lighted a fire in the room under the haunted one, and took off his boots and set them on the hearth, and stretched out his feet and warmed himself. For a time he prospered in his unbelief; but a little while after the night had fallen, and everything had got very dark, one of his boots began to move. It got up off the floor and gave a kind of slow jump towards the door, and then the other boot did the same, and after that the first boot jumped again. And thereupon it occurred to the man that an invisible being had got into his boots, and was now going away in them. When the boots reached the door they went upstairs slowly, and then the man heard them go tramp, tramp, round the haunted room over his head. A few minutes passed, and he could hear them again upon the stairs, and after that in the passage outside, and then one of them came in at the door, and the other gave a jump past it and came in too. They jumped along towards him, and then one got up and hit him, and afterwards the other hit him, and then again the first hit him, and so on, until they drove him out of the room, and finally out of the house. In this way he was kicked out by his own boots, and Donegal was avenged upon its doubter. It is not recorded whether the invisible being was a ghost or one of the Sidhe, but the fantastic nature of the vengeance is like the work of the Sidhe who live in the heart of fantasy.

A COWARD

ONE DAY I was at the house of my friend the strong farmer, who lives beyond Ben Bulben and Cope's mountain, and met there a young lad who seemed to be disliked by the two daughters. I asked why they disliked him, and was told he was a coward. This interested me, for some whom robust children of Nature take to be cowards are but men and women with a nervous system too finely made for their life and work. I looked at the lad; but no, that pink-and-white face and strong body had nothing of undue sensibility. After a little he told me his story. He had lived a wild and reckless life, until one day, two years before, he was coming home late at night, and suddenly felt himself sinking in, as it were, upon the ghostly world. For a moment he saw the face of a dead brother rise up before him, and then he turned and ran. He did not stop till he came to a cottage nearly a mile down the road. He flung himself against the door with so much of violence that he broke the thick wooden bolt and fell upon the floor. From that day he gave up his wild life, but was a hopeless coward. Nothing could ever bring him to look, either by day or night, upon the spot where he had seen the face, and he often went two miles round to avoid it; nor could, he said, 'the prettiest girl in the country' persuade him to see her home after a party if he were alone.

THE THREE O'BYRNES AND THE EVIL FAERIES

I N THE DIM kingdom there is a great abundance of all excellent things. There is more love there than upon the earth; there is more dancing there than upon the earth; and there is more treasure there than upon the earth. In the beginning the earth was perhaps made to fulfil the desire of man, but now it has got old and fallen into decay. What wonder if we try and pilfer the treasures of that other kingdom!

A friend was once at a village near Slieve League. One day he was straying about a rath called 'Cashel Nore'. A man with a haggard face and unkempt hair, and clothes falling in pieces, came into the rath and began digging. My friend turned to a peasant who was working near and asked who the man was. 'That is the third O'Byrne,' was the answer. A few days after he learned this story: A great quantity of treasure had been buried in the rath in pagan times, and a number of evil faeries set to guard it; but some day it was to be found and belong to the family of the O'Byrnes. Before that day three O'Byrnes must find it and die. Two had already done so. The first had dug and dug until at last he got a glimpse of the stone coffin that contained it, but immediately a thing like a huge hairy dog came down the mountain and tore him to pieces. The next morning the treasure had again vanished deep into the earth. The second O'Byrne came and dug and dug until he found the coffin, and lifted the lid and saw the gold shining within. He saw some horrible sight the next moment, and went raving mad and soon died. The treasure again sank out of sight. The third O'Byrne is now digging. He believes that he will die in some terrible way the moment he finds the treasure, but that the spell will be broken, and the O'Byrne family made rich for ever, as they were of old.

A peasant of the neighbourhood once saw the treasure. He found the shin-bone of a hare lying on the grass. He took it up; there was a hole in it; he looked through the hole, and saw the gold heaped up under the ground. He hurried home to bring a spade, but when he got to the rath again he could not find the spot where he had seen it.

—

DRUMCLIFF AND ROSSES

DRUMCLIFF AND ROSSES were, are, and ever shall be, please Heaven! places of unearthly resort. I have lived near by them and in them, time after time, and thereby gathered much faery lore. Drumcliff is a wide green valley, lying at the foot of Ben Bulben, whereon the great Saint Columba himself, the builder of many of the old ruins in the valley, climbed one day to get near Heaven with his prayers. Rosses is a little sea-dividing, sandy plain, covered with short grass, like a green table-cloth, and lying in the foam midway between the round cairn-headed Knocknarea and 'Ben Bulben, famous for hawks':

> But for Ben Bulben and Knocknarea
> Many a poor sailor'd be cast away,

as the rhyme goes.

At the northern corner of Rosses is a little promontory of sand and rocks and grass: a mournful, haunted place. Few countrymen would fall asleep under its low cliff, for he who sleeps here may wake 'silly', the Sidhe having carried off his soul. There is no more ready short-cut to the dim kingdom than this plovery headland, for, covered and smothered now from sight by mounds of sand, a long cave goes thither 'full of gold and silver, and the most beautiful parlours and drawing-rooms.' Once, before the sand covered it, a dog strayed in, and was heard yelping helplessly deep underground in a fort far inland. These forts or raths, made before modern history had begun, cover all Rosses and all Columcille. The one where the dog yelped has, like most others, an underground beehive chamber in the midst. Once when I was poking about there, an unusually intelligent and 'reading' countryman who had come with me, and waited outside, knelt down by the opening, and whispered in a timid voice, 'Are you all right, sir?' I had been some little while underground, and he feared I had been carried off like the dog.

This fort or rath is on the ridge of a small hill, on whose northern slope lie a few stray cottages. One night a farmer's young son came from one of them and saw it all flaming, and ran towards it, but the 'glamour' fell on him, and he sprang on to a fence, cross-legged, and commenced beating it with a stick, for he imagined the fence was a horse. In the morning he was still beating his fence, still riding across country as it seemed to him, and they carried him home, where he remained a simpleton for three years before he came to himself again. A little later a farmer tried to level the fort. His cows and horses died, and all manner of trouble overtook him, and finally he himself was led home, and left useless with 'his head on his knees by the fire to the day of his death.'

A few hundred yards southwards of the northern angle of Rosses is another angle having also its cave, though this one is not covered with sand. About twenty years ago a brig was wrecked near by, and three or four fishermen were put to watch the deserted hulk through the darkness. At midnight they saw sitting on a stone at the cave's mouth two red-capped fiddlers fiddling with all their might. The men fled. A great crowd of villagers rushed down to the cave to see the fiddlers, but the creatures had gone.

To the wise peasant the green hills and woods round him are full of never-fading mystery. When the aged country-woman stands at her door in the evening, and, in her own words, 'looks at the mountains and thinks of the goodness of God,' God is all the nearer, because the pagan powers are not far: because northward in Ben Bulben, famous for hawks, the white square door swings open at sundown, and those wild unchristian riders rush forth upon the fields, while southward the White Lady, who is doubtless Maeve herself, wanders under the broad cloud nightcap of Knocknarea. How may she doubt these things, even though the priest shakes his head at her? Did not a herd-boy, no long while since, see the White Lady? She passed so close that the skirt of her dress touched him. 'He fell down, and was dead three days.'

One night as I sat eating Mrs. H——'s soda-bread, her husband told me a longish story, much the best of all I heard in Rosses. Many a poor man from Finn mac Cumhal to our own days has had some such adventure to tell of, for the 'Good People' love to repeat themselves. At any rate the story-tellers do. 'In the times when, we used to travel by the canal,' he said, 'I was coming down from Dublin. When we came to Mullingar the canal ended, and I began to walk, and stiff and fatigued I was after the slowness. I had some friends with me, and now and then we walked, now and then we rode in a cart. So on till we saw some girls milking cows, and stopped to joke with them. After a while we asked them for a drink of milk. "We have nothing to put it in here," they said, "but come to the house with us." We went home with them, and sat round the fire talking. After a while the others went, and left me, loath to stir from the good fire. I asked the girls for something to eat. There was a pot on the fire, and they took the meat out and put it on a plate, and told me to eat only the meat that came off the head. When I had eaten, the girls went out, and I did not see them again. It grew darker and darker, and there I still sat, loath as ever to leave the good fire, and after a while two men came in, carrying between them a corpse. When I saw them coming I hid behind the door. Says one to the other, putting the corpse on the spit. "Who'll turn the meat?" Says the other, "Michael H——, come out of that and turn the meat." I came out all of a tremble, and began turning the corpse. "Michael H——," says the one who spoke first, "if you let it burn we'll have to put you on the spit instead"; and on that they went out. I sat there trembling and turning the corpse till towards midnight. The men came again, and the one said it was burnt, and the other said it was done right. But having fallen out over it, they both said they would do me no harm that time; and, sitting by the fire, one of them cried out: "Michael H——, can you tell me a story?" "Divil a one," said I. On which he caught me by the shoulder, and put me out like a shot. It was a wild blowing night. Never in all my born days did I see such a night—the darkest night that ever came out of the heavens. I did not know where I was for the life of me. So when one of the men came after me and touched me on the shoulder, with a "Micheal H——, can you tell a story now?" "I can," says I. In he brought me; and putting me by the fire, says, "Begin." "I have no story but the one," says I, "that I was sitting here, and you two men brought in a corpse and put it on the spit, and set me turning it."

'I sat trembling and turning the corpse until midnight.'

"That will do," says he; "ye may go in there and lie down on the bed." And I went, nothing loath; and in the morning where was I but in the middle of a green field!'

Drumcliff is a great place for omens. Before a prosperous fishing season a herring-barrel appears in the midst of a storm-cloud; and at a place called Columcille's Strand, a place of marsh and mire, an ancient boat, with Saint Columba himself, comes floating in from sea on a moonlight night; a portent of a brave harvesting. They have their dread portents too. Some few seasons ago a fisherman saw, far on the horizon, renowned Hy Brazil, where he who touches shall find no more labour or care, nor cynic laughter, but shall go walking about under shadiest boscage, and enjoy the conversation of Cuchulaın and his heroes. A vision of Hy Brazil forebodes national troubles.

Drumcliff and Rosses are choke-full of ghosts. By bog, road, rath, hillside, sea-border they gather in all shapes: headless women, men in armour, shadow hares, fire-tongued hounds, whistling seals, and so on. A whistling seal sank a ship the other day. At Drumcliff there is a very ancient graveyard. *The Annals of the Four Masters* have this verse about a soldier named Denadhach, who died in 871: 'A pious soldier of the race of Conn lies under hazel crosses at Drumcliff.' Not very long ago an old woman, turning to go into the churchyard at night to pray, saw standing before her a man in armour, who asked her where she was going. It was the 'pious soldier of the race of Conn', says local wisdom, still keeping watch, with his ancient piety, over the graveyard. Again, the custom is still common hereabouts of sprinkling the doorstep with the blood of a chicken on the death of a very young child, thus (as the belief is) drawing into the blood the evil spirits from the too weak soul. Blood is a great gatherer of evil spirits. To cut your hand on a stone on going into a fort is said to be very dangerous.

There is no more curious ghost in Drumcliff or Rosses than the snipe-ghost. There is a bush behind a house in a village that I know well: for excellent reasons I do not say whether in Drumcliff or Rosses or on the slope of Ben Bulben, or even on the plain round Knocknarea. There is a history concerning the house and the bush. A man once lived there who found on the quay of Sligo a package containing three hundred pounds in notes. It was dropped by a foreign sea-captain. This my man knew, but said nothing. It was money for freight, and the sea-captain, not daring to face his owners, committed suicide in mid-ocean. Shortly afterwards my man died. His soul could not rest. At any rate, strange sounds were heard round his house. The wife was often seen by those still alive out in the garden praying at the bush I have spoken of, for the shade of the dead man appeared there at times. The bush remains to this day: once portion of a hedge, it now stands by itself, for no one dare put spade or pruning-knife about it. As to the strange sounds and voices, they did not cease till a few

The man in armour in the churchyard

years ago, when, during some repairs, a snipe flew out of the solid plaster and away; the troubled ghost, say the neighbours, of the note-finder was at last dislodged.

My forebears and relations have lived at Rosses and Drumcliff these many years. A few miles northward I am wholly a stranger, and can find nothing. When I ask for stories of the faeries, my answer is some such as was given me by a woman who lives near a white stone fort —one of the few stone ones in Ireland—under the seaward angle of Ben Bulben: 'They always mind their own affairs and I always mind mine': for it is dangerous to talk of them. Only friendship for yourself or knowledge of your forebears will loosen these cautious tongues. One friend of mine (I do not give his name for fear of gaugers) has the science of unpacking the stubbornest heart, but then he supplies the potheen-makers with grain from his own fields. Besides, he is descended from a noted Gaelic magician, and he has a kind of prescriptive right to hear tell of all kinds of other-world creatures. They are relations of his, if all people say concerning the parentage of magicians be true.

THE THICK SKULL OF THE FORTUNATE

I

ONCE A NUMBER of Icelandic peasantry found a very thick skull in the cemetery where the poet Egil was buried. Its great thickness made them feel certain it was the skull of a great man, doubtless of Egil himself. To be doubly sure they put it on a wall and hit it hard blows with a hammer. It got white where the blows fell, but did not break, and they were convinced that it was in truth the skull of the poet, and worthy of every honour. In Ireland we have much kinship with the Icelanders, or 'Danes' as we call them, and all other dwellers in the Scandinavian countries. In some of our mountainous and barren places, and in our seaboard villages, we still test each other in much the same way the Icelanders tested the head of Egil. We may have acquired the custom from those ancient Danish pirates, whose descendants, the people of Rosses tell me, still remember every field and hillock in Ireland which once belonged to their forebears, and are able to describe Rosses itself as well as any native. There is one seaboard district known as Roughley, where the men are never known to shave or trim their wild red beards, and where there is a fight ever on foot. I have seen them at a boat-race fall foul of each other, and after much loud Gaelic, strike each other with oars. The first boat had gone aground, and by dint of hitting out with the long oars kept the second boat from passing, only to give the victory to the third. One day, the Sligo people say, a man from Roughley was tried in Sligo for breaking a skull in a row, and made the defence, not unknown in Ireland, that some heads are so thin you cannot be responsible for them. Having turned with a look of passionate contempt towards the solicitor who was prosecuting, and cried, 'That little fellow's skull if ye were to hit it would go like an egg-shell,' he beamed upon the judge, and said in a wheedling voice, 'but a man might wallop away at your lordship's for a fortnight.'

II

I wrote all this years ago, out of what were even then old memories. I was in Roughley the other day, and found it much like other desolate places. I may have been thinking of Moughorow, a much wilder place, for the memories of one's childhood are brittle things to lean upon.

1902.

THE RELIGION OF A SAILOR

A SEA-CAPTAIN when he stands upon the bridge, or looks out from his deck-house, thinks much about God and about the world. Away in the valley yonder among the corn and the poppies men may well forget all things except the warmth of the sun upon the face, and the kind shadow under the hedge; but he who journeys through storm and darkness must needs think and think. One July a couple of years ago I took my supper with a Captain Moran on board the s.s. *Margaret*, that had put into a western river from I know not where. I found him a man of many notions all flavoured with his personality, as is the way with sailors.

'Sur,' said he, 'did you ever hear tell of the sea-captain's prayer?'

'No,' said I; 'what is it?'

'It is,' he replied, ' "O Lord, give me a stiff upper lip." '

'And what does that mean?'

'It means,' he said, 'that when they come to me some night and wake me up, and say, "Captain, we're going down," that I won't make a fool o' meself. Why, sur, we war in mid Atlantic, and I standin' on the bridge, when the third mate comes up to me lookin' mortial bad. Says he, "Captain, all's up with us." Says I, "Didn't you know when you joined that a certain percentage go down every year?" "Yes, sur," says he; and says I, "Aren't you paid to go down?" "Yes, sur," says he; and says I, "Then go down like a man, and be damned to you!" '

CONCERNING THE NEARNESS TOGETHER OF
HEAVEN, EARTH, AND PURGATORY

IN IRELAND this world and the world we go to after death are not far apart. I have heard of a ghost that was many years in a tree and many years in the archway of a bridge, and my old Mayo woman says, 'There is a bush up at my own place, and the people do be saying that there are two souls doing their penance under it. When the wind blows one way the one has shelter, and when it blows from the north the other one has shelter. It is twisted over with the way they be rooting under it for shelter. I don't believe it, but there is many a one would not pass by it at night.' Indeed there are times when the worlds are so near together that it seems as if our earthly chattels were no more than the shadows of things beyond. A lady I knew once saw a village child running about with a long trailing petticoat upon her, and asked why she did not have it cut short. 'It was my grandmother's,' said the child; 'would you have her going about yonder with her petticoat up to her knees, and she dead but four days?' I have read the story of a woman whose ghost haunted her people because they had made her grave-clothes so short that the fires of Purgatory burned her knees. The peasantry expect to have beyond the grave houses much like their earthly houses, only there the thatch will never grow leaky, nor the white walls lose their lustre, nor shall the dairy be at any time empty of good milk and butter. But now and then a landlord or an agent or a gauger will go by begging for bread, to show how God divides the righteous from the unrighteous.

1892 and 1902.

THE EATERS OF PRECIOUS STONES

SOMETIMES when I have been shut off from common interests, and have for a little forgotten to be restless, I get waking dreams, now faint and shadow-like, now vivid and solid-looking, like the material world under my feet. Whether they be faint or vivid, they are ever beyond the power of my will to alter in any way. They have their own will, and sweep hither and thither, and change according to its commands. One day I saw faintly an immense pit of blackness, round which went a circular parapet, and on this parapet sat innumerable apes eating precious stones out of the palms of their hands. The stones glittered green and crimson, and the apes devoured them with an insatiable hunger. I knew that I saw my own Hell there, the Hell of the artist, and that all who sought after beautiful and wonderful things with too avid a thirst, lost peace and form and became shapeless and common. I have seen into other people's Hells also, and saw in one an infernal Peter, who had a black face and white lips, and who weighed on a curious double scales not only the evil deeds committed, but the good deeds left undone, of certain invisible shades. I could see the scales go up and down, but I could not see the shades who were, I knew, crowding about him. I saw on another occasion a quantity of demons of all kinds of shapes—fish-like, serpent-like, ape-like, and dog-like—sitting about a black pit such as that in my own Hell, and looking at the moon-like reflection of the heavens which shone up from the depths of the pit.

OUR LADY OF THE HILLS

WHEN WE WERE children we did not say 'at such a distance from the post-office,' or 'so far from the butcher's or the grocer's', but measured things by the covered well in the wood, or by the burrow of the fox in the hill. We belonged to God and to His works, and to things come down from the ancient days. We would not have been greatly surprised had we met the shining feet of an angel among the white mushrooms upon the mountains, for we knew in those days immense despair, unfathomed love—every eternal mood,—but now the draw-net is about our feet. A few miles eastward of Lough Gill, a young Protestant girl, who was both pretty herself and prettily dressed in blue and white, wandered up among those mountain mushrooms, and I have a letter of hers telling how she met a troop of children, and became a portion of their dream. When they first saw her they threw themselves face down in a bed of rushes, as if in a great fear; but after a little other children came about them, and they got up and followed her almost bravely. She noticed their fear, and presently stood still and held out her arms. A little girl threw herself into them with the cry, 'Ah, you are the Virgin out o' the picture!' 'No,' said another, coming near also, 'she is a sky faery, for she has the colour of the sky.' 'No,' said a third, 'she is the faery out of the foxglove grown big.' The other children, however, would have it that she was indeed the Virgin, for she wore the Virgin's colours. Her good Protestant heart was greatly troubled, and she got the children to sit down about her, and tried to explain who she was, but they would have none of her explanation. Finding explanation of no avail, she asked had they ever heard of Christ? 'Yes,' said one; 'but we do not like Him, for He would kill us if it were not for the Virgin.' 'Tell Him to be good to me,' whispered another into her ear. 'He would not let me near Him, for dad says I am a divil,' burst out a third.

She talked to them a long time about Christ and the apostles, but was finally interrupted by an elderly woman with a stick, who, taking her to be some adventurous hunter for converts, drove the children away, despite their explanations that here was the great Queen of Heaven come to walk upon the mountain and be kind to them. When the children had gone she went on her way, and had walked about half a mile, when the child who was called 'a divil' jumped down from the high ditch by the lane, and said she would believe her 'an ordinary lady' if she had 'two skirts', for 'ladies always had two skirts.' The 'two skirts' were shown, and the child went away crestfallen, but a few minutes later jumped down again from the ditch, and cried angrily, 'Dad's a divil, mum's a divil, and I'm a divil, and you are only an ordinary lady,' and having flung a handful of mud and pebbles ran away sobbing. When my pretty Protestant had come to her own home she found that she had dropped the tassels of her parasol. A year later she was by chance upon the mountain, but wearing now a plain black dress, and met the child who had first called her the Virgin out o' the picture, and saw the tassels hanging about the child's neck, and said, 'I am the lady you met last year, who told you about Christ.' 'No, you are not! no, you are not! no, you are not!' was the passionate reply.

THE GOLDEN AGE

A WHILE AGO I was in the train, and getting near Sligo. The last time I had been there something was troubling me, and I had longed for a message from those beings or bodiless moods, or whatever they may be, who inhabit the world of spirits. The message came, for one night I saw with blinding distinctness, as I lay between sleeping and waking, a black animal, half weasel, half dog, moving along the top of a stone wall, and presently the black animal vanished, and from the other side came a white weasel-like dog, his pink flesh shining through his white hair and all in a blaze of light; and I remembered a peasant belief about two faery dogs who go about representing day and night, good and evil, and was comforted by the excellent omen. But now I longed for a message of another kind, and chance, if chance there is, brought it, for a man got into the carriage and began to play on a fiddle made apparently of an old blacking-box, and though I am quite unmusical the sounds filled me with the strangest emotions. I seemed to hear a voice of lamentation out of the Golden Age. It told me that we are imperfect, incomplete, and no more like a beautiful woven web, but like a bundle of cords knotted together and flung into a corner. It said that the world was once all perfect and kindly, and that still the kindly and perfect world existed, but buried like a mass of roses under many spadefuls of earth. The faeries and the more innocent of the spirits dwelt within it, and lamented over our fallen world in the lamentation of the wind-tossed reeds, in the song of the birds, in the moan of the waves, and in the sweet cry of the fiddle. It said that with us the beautiful are not clever and the clever are not beautiful, and that the best of our moments are marred by a little vulgarity, or by a needle-prick out of sad recollection, and that the fiddle must ever lament about it. It said that if only they who live in the Golden Age could die we might be happy, for the sad voices would be still; but they must sing and we must weep until the eternal gates swing open.

A REMONSTRANCE WITH SCOTSMEN FOR HAVING SOURED THE DISPOSITION OF THEIR GHOSTS AND FAERIES

NOT ONLY IN Ireland is faery belief still extant. It was only the other day I heard of a Scottish farmer who believed that the lake in front of his house was haunted by a water-horse. He was afraid of it, and dragged the lake with nets, and then tried to pump it empty. It would have been a bad thing for the water-horse had he found him. An Irish peasant would have long since come to terms with the creature. For in Ireland there is something of timid affection between men and spirits. They only ill-treat each other in reason; each admits the other to have feelings. There are points beyond which neither will go. No Irish peasant would treat a captured faery as did the man Campbell tells of. He caught a kelpie, and tied her behind him on his horse. She was fierce, but he kept her quiet by driving an awl and a needle into her. They came to a river, and she grew very restless, fearing to cross the water. Again he drove the awl and needle into her. She cried out, 'Pierce me with the awl, but keep that slender, hair-like slave (the needle) out of me.' They came to an inn. He turned the light of a lantern on her; immediately she dropped down 'like a falling star', and changed into a lump of jelly. She was dead. Nor would they treat the faeries as one is treated in an old Highland poem. A faery loved a little child who used to cut turf at the side of a faery hill. Every day the faery put out his hand from the hill with an enchanted knife. The child used to cut the turf with the knife. It did not take long, the knife being charmed. Her brothers wondered why she was done so quickly. At last they resolved to watch, and find out who helped her. They saw the small hand come out of the earth, and the little child take from it the knife. When the turf was all cut, they saw her make three taps on the ground with the handle. The small hand came out of the hill. Snatching the knife from the child, they cut the hand off with a blow. The faery was never again seen. He drew his bleeding arm into the earth, thinking, as it is recorded, he had lost his hand through the treachery of the child.

In Scotland you are too theological, too gloomy. You have even made the Devil religious. 'Where do you live, good-wyf, and how is the minister?' he said to the witch when he met her on the high-road, as it came out in the trial. You have burnt all the witches. In Ireland we have left them alone. To be sure, the 'loyal minority' knocked out the eye of one with a cabbage-stump on the 31st of March 1711, in the town of Carrickfergus. But then the 'loyal minority' is half Scottish. You have discovered the faeries to be pagan and wicked. You would like to have them all up before the magistrate. In Ireland warlike mortals have gone among them, and helped them in their battles, and they in turn have taught men great skill with herbs, and permitted some few to hear their tunes. Carolan slept upon a faery rath. Ever after their tunes ran in his head, and made him the great musician he was. In Scotland you have denounced them from the pulpit. In Ireland they have been permitted by the priests to consult them on the state of their souls. Unhappily the priests have decided that they have no souls, that they will dry up like so much bright vapour at the last day; but more in sadness than in anger. The Catholic religion likes to keep on good terms with its neighbours.

These two different ways of looking at things have influenced in each country the whole world of sprites and goblins. For their gay and graceful doings you must go to Ireland; for their deeds of terror to Scotland. Our Irish faery terrors have about them something of make-believe. When a countryman strays into an enchanted hovel, and is made to turn a corpse all night on a spit before the fire, we do not feel anxious; we

125

know he will wake in the midst of a green field, the dew on his old coat. In Scotland it is altogether different. You have soured the naturally excellent disposition of ghosts and goblins. The piper M'Crimmon of the Hebrides shouldered his pipes and marched into a sea cavern, playing loudly, and followed by his dog. For a long time the people could hear the pipes. He must have gone nearly a mile, when they heard the sound of a struggle. Then the piping ceased suddenly. Some time went by, and then his dog came out of the cavern completely flayed, too weak even to howl. Nothing else ever came out of the cavern. Then there is the tale of the man who dived into a lake where treasure was thought to be. He saw a great coffer of iron. Close to the coffer lay a monster, who warned him to return whence he came. He rose to the surface; but the bystanders, when they heard he had seen the treasure, persuaded him to dive again. He dived. In a little while his heart and liver floated up, reddening the water. No man ever saw the rest of his body.

These water-goblins and water-monsters are common in Scottish folk-lore. We have them too, but take them much less dreadfully. A hole in the Sligo river is haunted by one of these monsters. He is ardently believed in by many, but that does not prevent the country-people playing with subject, and surrounding it with deliberate fantasy. When I was a small boy I fished one day for congers in the monster's hole. Returning home, a great eel on my shoulder, his head flapping down in front, his tail sweeping the ground behind, I met a fisherman of my acquaintance. I began a tale of an immense conger, three times larger than the one I carried, that had broken my line and escaped. 'That was him,' said the fisherman. 'Did you ever hear how he made my brother emigrate? My brother was a diver, as you know, and grubbed stones for the Harbour Board. One day the beast comes up to him, and says, "What are you after?" "Stones, sur," says he. "Don't you think you had better be going?" "Yes, sur," says he. And that's why my brother emigrated.

WAR

WHEN THERE was a rumour of war with France a while ago, I met a poor Sligo woman, a soldier's widow, that I know, and I read her a sentence out of a letter I had just had from London: 'The people here are mad for war, but France seems inclined to take things peacefully,' or some like sentence. Her mind ran a good deal on war, which she imagined partly from what she had heard from soldiers, and partly from tradition of the rebellion of '98, but the word London doubled her interest, for she knew there were a great many people in London, and she herself had once lived in 'a congested district'. 'There are too many over one another in London. They are getting tired of the world. It is killed they want to be. It will be no matter; but sure the French want nothing but peace and quietness. The people here don't mind the war coming. They could not be worse than they are. They may as well die soldierly before God. Sure they will get quarters in Heaven.' Then she began to say that it would be a hard thing to see children tossed about on bayonets, and I knew her mind was running on traditions of the great rebellion. She said presently, 'I never knew a man that was in a battle that liked to speak of it after. They'd sooner be throwing hay down from a hayrick.' She told me how she and her neighbours used to be sitting over the fire when she was a girl, talking of the war that was coming, and now she was afraid it was coming again, for she had dreamed that all the bay was 'stranded and covered with seaweed.' I asked her if it was in the Fenian times that she had been so much afraid of war coming. But she cried out,

'Never had I such fun and pleasure as in the Fenian times. I was in a house where some of the officers used to be staying, and in the daytime I would be walking after the soldiers' band, and at night I'd be going down to the end of the garden watching a soldier, with his red coat on him, drilling the Fenians in the field behind the house. One night the boys tied the liver of an old horse, that had been dead three weeks, to the knocker, and I found it when I opened the door in the morning.' And presently our talk of war shifted, as it had a way of doing, to the battle of the Black Pig, which seems to her a battle between Ireland and England, but to me an Armageddon which shall quench all things in the Ancestral Darkness again, and from this to sayings about war and vengeance. 'Do you know,' she said, 'what the curse of the Four Fathers is? They put the man-child on the spear, and somebody said to them, "You will be cursed in the fourth generation after you," and that is why disease or anything always come in the fourth generation.'

1902.

THE QUEEN AND THE FOOL

I HAVE HEARD one Hearne, a witch-doctor, who is on the border of Clare and Galway, say that in 'every household' of Faery 'there is a queen and a fool', and that if you are 'touched' by either you never recover, though you may from the touch of any other in Faery. He said of the fool that he was 'maybe the wisest of all', and spoke of him as dressed like one of 'the mummers that used to be going about the country.' I remember seeing a long, lank, ragged man sitting by the hearth in the cottage of an old miller not far from where I am now writing, and being told that he was a fool; and from the stories that a friend has gathered for me I find that he is believed to go to Faery in his sleep; but whether he becomes an *Amadán-na-Breena*, a fool of the forth, and is attached to a household there, I cannot tell. It was an old woman that I know well, and who has been in Faery herself, that spoke to my friend about him. She said, 'There are fools amongst them, and the fools we see, like that *Amadán* of Ballylee, go away with them at night, and so do the woman fools that we call *Oinseachs* (apes).' A woman who is related to the witch-doctor on the border of Clare, and who can cure people and cattle by spells, said, 'There are some cures I can't do. I can't help any one that has got a stroke from the queen or the fool of the forth. I knew of a woman that saw the queen one time, and she looked like any Christian. I never heard of any that saw the fool but one woman that was walking near Gort, and she said, "There is the fool of the forth coming after me." So her friends that were with her called out, though they could see nothing, and I suppose he went away at that, for she got no harm. He was like a big strong man, she said, and half naked, and that is all she said about him. I have never seen any myself, but I am a cousin of Hearne, and my uncle was away twenty-one years.' The wife of the old miller said, 'It is said they are mostly good neighbours, but the stroke of the fool is what there is no cure for; any one that gets that is gone. The *Amadán-na-Breena* we call him!' And an old woman who lives in the Bog of Kiltartan, and is very poor, said, 'It is true enough, there is no cure for the stroke of the *Amadán-na-Breena*. There was an old man I knew long ago, he had a tape, and he could tell what diseases you had with measuring you; and he knew many things. And he said to me at one time, "What month of the year is the worst?" and I said, "The month of May, of course," "It is not," he said; "but the month of June, for that's the month that the *Amadán* gives his stroke!" They say he looks like any other man, but he's *leathan* (wide), and not smart. I knew a boy one time got a great fright, for a lamb looked over the wall at him with a beard on it, and he knew it was the *Amadán*, for it was the month of June. And they brought him to that man I was telling you about, that had the tape, and when he saw him he said, "Send for the priest, and get a Mass said over him." And so they did, and what would you say but he's living yet and has a family! A certain Regan said, "They, the other sort of people, might be passing you close here and they might touch you. But any that gets the touch of the *Amadán-na-Breena* is done for." It's true enough that it's in the month of June he's most likely to give the touch. I knew one that got it, and he told me about it himself. He was a boy I knew well, and he told me that one night a gentleman came to him, that had been his land-lord, and that was dead. And he told him to come along with him, for he wanted him to fight another man. And when he went he found two great troops of them, and the other troop had a living man with them too, and he was put to fight him. And they had a great fight, and he got the better of the other man, and then the troop on his side gave a great shout, and he was let home again. But about three years

'That love, when limbs are interwoven'

after that he was cutting bushes in a wood and he saw the *Amadán* coming at him. He had a big vessel in his arms, and it was shining, so that the boy could see nothing else; but he put it behind his back then and came running, and the boy said he looked wild and wide, like the side of the hill. And the boy ran, and he threw the vessel after him, and it broke with a great noise, and whatever came out of it, his head was gone there and then. He lived for a while after, and used to tell us many things, but his wits were gone. He thought they mightn't have liked him to beat the other man, and he used to be afraid something would come on him.' And an old woman in Galway workhouse, who had some little knowledge of Queen Maeve, said the other day, 'The *Amadán-na-Breena* changes his shape every two days. Sometimes he comes like a youngster, and then he'll come like the worst of beasts, trying to give the touch he used to be. I heard it said of late he was shot, but I think myself it would be hard to shoot him.'

I knew a man who was trying to bring before his mind's eye an image of Aengus, the old Irish god of love and poetry and ecstasy, who changed four of his kisses into birds, and suddenly the image of a man with a cap and bells rushed before his mind's eye, and grew vivid and spoke and called itself 'Aengus' messenger'. And I knew another man, a truly great seer, who saw a white fool in a visionary garden, where there was a tree with peacocks' feathers instead of leaves, and flowers that opened to show little human faces when the white fool had touched them with his cockscomb, and he saw at another time a white fool sitting by a pool and smiling and watching images of beautiful women floating up from the pool.

What else can death be but the beginning of wisdom and power and beauty? and foolishness may be a kind of death. I cannot think it wonderful that many should see a fool with a shining vessel of some enchantment or wisdom or dream too powerful for mortal brains in 'every household of them'. It is natural, too, that there should be a queen to every household of them, and that one should hear little of their kings, for women come more easily than men to that wisdom which

ancient peoples, and all wild peoples even now, think the only wisdom. The self, which is the foundation of our knowledge, is broken in pieces by foolishness, and is forgotten in the sudden emotions of women, and therefore fools may get, and women do get of a certainty, glimpses of much that sanctity finds at the end of its painful journey. The man who saw the white fool said of a certain woman, not a peasant woman, 'If I had her power of vision I would know all the wisdom of the gods, and her visions do not interest her.' And I know of another woman, also not a peasant woman, who would pass in sleep into countries of an unearthly beauty, and who never cared for anything but to be busy about her house and her children; and presently a herb doctor cured her, as he called it. Wisdom and beauty and power may sometimes, as I think, come to those who die every day they live, though their dying may not be like the dying Shakespeare spoke of. There is a war between the living and the dead, and the Irish stories keep harping upon it. They will have it that when the potatoes or the wheat or any other of the fruits of the earth decay, they ripen in Faery, and that our dreams lose their wisdom when the sap rises in the trees, and that our dreams can make the trees wither, and that one hears the bleating of the lambs of Faery in November, and that blind eyes can see more than other eyes. Because the soul always believes in these, or in like things, the cell and the wilderness shall never be long empty, or lovers come into the world who will not understand the verse:—

> Heardst thou not sweet words among
> That heaven-resounding minstrelsy?
> Heardst thou not that those who die
> Awake in a world of ecstasy?
> That love, when limbs are interwoven,
> And sleep when the night of life is cloven,
> And thought, to the world's dim boundaries clinging,
> And music, when one beloved is singing,
> Is death?

1901.

134

THE FRIENDS OF THE PEOPLE OF FAERY

THOSE THAT see the people of Faery most often, and so have the most of their wisdom, are often very poor, but often, too, they are thought to have a strength beyond that of man, as though one came, when one has passed the threshold of trance, to those sweet waters where Maeldun saw the dishevelled eagles bathe and become young again.

There was an old Martin Roland, who lived near a bog a little out of Gort, who saw them often from his young days, and always towards the end of his life, though I would hardly call him their friend. He told me a few months before his death that 'they' would not let him sleep at night with crying things at him in Irish, and with playing their pipes. He had asked a friend of his what he should do, and the friend had told him to buy a flute, and play on it when they began to shout or to play on their pipes, and maybe they would give up annoying him; and he did, and they always went out into the field when he began to play. He showed me the pipe, and blew through it, and made a noise, but he did not know how to play; and then he showed me where he had pulled his chimney down, because one of them used to sit up on it and play on the pipes. A friend of his and mine went to see him a little time ago, for she heard that 'three of them' had told him he was to die. He said they had gone away after warning him, and that the children (children they had 'taken', I suppose) who used to come with them, and play about the house with them, had 'gone to some other place', because 'they found the house too cold for them, maybe'; and he died a week after he had said these things.

His neighbours were not certain that he really saw anything in his old age, but they were all certain that he saw things when he was a young man. His brother said, 'Old he is, and it's all in his brain the things he sees. If he was a young man we might believe in him.' But he was improvident, and never got on with his brothers. A neighbour said, 'The poor man! They say they are mostly in his head now, but sure he was a fine fresh man twenty years ago the night he saw them linked in two lots, like young slips of girls walking together. It was the night they took away Fallon's little girl.' And she told how Fallon's little girl had met a woman 'with red hair that was as bright as silver', who took her away. Another neighbour, who was herself 'clouted over the ear' by one of them for going into a fort where they were, said, 'I believe it's mostly in his head they are; and when he stood in the door last night I said, "The wind does be always in my ears, and the sound of it never stops", to make him think it was the same with him; but he says, "I hear them singing and making music all the time, and one of them is after bringing out a little flute, and it's on it he's playing to them." And this I know, that when he pulled down the chimney where he said the piper used to be sitting and playing, he lifted up stones, and he an old man, that I could not have lifted when I was young and strong.'

A friend has sent me from Ulster an account of one who was on terms of true friendship with the people of Faery. It has been taken down accurately, for my friend, who had heard the old woman's story some time before I heard of it, got her to tell it over again, and wrote it out at once. She began by telling the old woman that she did not like being in the house alone because of the ghosts and faeries; and the old woman said, 'There's nothing to be frightened about in faeries, Miss. Many's the time I talked to a woman myself that was a faery, or something of the sort, and no less and more than mortal anyhow. She used to come about your grandfather's house—your mother's grandfather, that is—in my young days. But you'll have heard all about her.' My friend said that she had heard about her, but a long time before, and she wanted to hear about her again; and the old woman went on, 'Well, dear, the very first time ever I heard word of her coming about was when your uncle—that is, your mother's uncle—Joseph married, and was building a house for his wife, for he brought her first to his father's, up at the house by the Lough. My father and us were living nigh-hand to where the new house was to be built, to overlook the men at their work. My father was a weaver, and brought his looms and all there into a cottage that was close by. The foundations were marked out, and the building stones lying about, but the masons had not come yet; and one day I was standing with my mother fornent the house, when we sees a smart wee woman coming up the field over the burn to us. I was a bit of a girl at the time, playing about and sporting myself, but I mind her as well as if I saw her there now!' My friend asked how the woman was dressed, and the old woman said, 'It was a grey cloak she had on, with a green cashmere skirt and a black silk hankercher tied round her head, like the countrywomen did use to wear in them times.' My friend asked, 'How wee was she?' And the old woman said, 'Well, now, she wasn't wee at all when I think of it, for all we called her the Wee Woman. She was bigger than many a one, and yet not tall as you would say. She was like a woman about thirty, brown-haired and round in the face. She was like Miss Betty, your grandmother's sister, and Betty was like none of the rest, not like your grandmother, nor any of them. She was round and fresh in the face, and she never was married, and she never would take any man; and we used to say that the Wee Woman—her being like Betty—was, maybe, one of their own people that had been took off before she grew to her full height, and for that she was always following us and warning and foretelling. This time she walks straight over to where my mother was standing. "Go over to the Lough this minute!"—ordering her like that—"Go over to the Lough, and tell Joseph that he must change the foundation of this house to where I'll show you fornent the thorn-bush. That is where it is to be built, if he is to have luck and prosperity, so do what I'm telling ye this minute." The house was being built on "the path", I suppose—the path used by the people of Faery on their journeys, and my mother brings Joseph down and shows him, and he changes the foundation, the way he was bid, but didn't bring it exactly to where was pointed, and the end of that was, when he come to the house, his own wife lost her life with an accident that come to a horse that hadn't room to turn right with a harrow between the bush and the wall. The Wee Woman was queer and angry when next she come, and says to us, "He didn't do as I bid him, but he'll see what he'll see." ' My friend asked where the woman came from this time, and if she was dressed as before, and the woman said, 'Always the same way, up the field beyant the burn. It was a thin sort of shawl she had about her in summer, and a cloak about her in winter; and many and many a time she came, and always it was good advice she was giving to my mother, and warning her what not to do if she would have good luck. There was none of the other children of us ever seen her unless me; but I used to be glad when I seen her coming up the burn, and would run out and catch her by the hand and the cloak, and call to my mother, "Here's the Wee Woman!" No man-body ever seen her. My father used to be wanting to, and was angry with my mother and me, thinking we were telling lies and talking foolish-like. And so one day when she had come, and was sitting by the fireside talking to my mother, I slips out to the field where he was digging. "Come up," says I, "if ye want to see her. She's sitting at the fireside now, talking to mother." So in he comes with me and looks round angry-like and sees nothing, and he up with a broom that was near hand and hits me a crig with it. "Take that now!" says he, "for making a fool of me!" and away with him as fast as he could, and queer and angry with me. The Wee Woman says to me then, "Ye got that now for bringing people to see me. No man-body ever seen me, and none ever will."

'There was one day, though, she gave him a queer fright anyway, whether he had seen her or not. He was in among the cattle when it happened, and he comes up to the house all trembling-like. "Don't let me hear you say another word of your Wee Woman. I have got enough of her this time." Another time, all the same, he was up Gortin to sell horses, and before he went off, in steps the Wee Woman and says she to my mother, holding out a sort of weed, "Your man is gone up by Gortin, and there's a bad fright waiting him coming home, but take this and sew it in his coat, and he'll get no harm by it." My mother takes the herb, but thinks to herself, "Sure, there's nothing in it", and throws it on the fire, and lo and behold, and sure enough! coming home from Gortin, my father got as bad a fright as ever he got in his life. What it was I don't right mind, but anyway he was badly damaged by it. My mother was in a queer way, frightened of the Wee Woman, after what she done, and sure enough the next time she was angry. "Ye didn't believe me," she said, "and ye threw the herb I gave ye in the fire, and I went far enough for it." There was another time she came and told how William Hearne was dead in America. "Go over," she says, "to the Lough, and say that William is dead, and he died happy, and this was the last Bible chapter ever he read", and with that she gave the verse and chapter. "Go," she says, "and tell them to read them at the next class-meeting, and that I held his head while he died." And sure enough word came after that how William had died on the day she named. And, doing as she bid about the chapter and the hymn, they never had such a prayer-meeting as that. One day she and me and my mother was standing talking, and she was warning her about something, when she says of a sudden, "Here comes Miss Letty in all her finery, and it's time for me to be off." And with that she gave a swirl round on her feet, and raises up in the air, and round and round she goes, and up and up, as if it was a winding stairs she went up, only far swifter.* She went up and up, till she was no bigger than a bird up against the clouds, singing and singing the whole time the loveliest music I ever heard in my life from that day to

* A countryman near Coole told me of a spirit so ascending. Swedenborg, in his *Spiritual Diary*, speaks of gyres of spirits, and Blake painted Jacob's Ladder as an ascending gyre.   1924.

this. It wasn't a hymn she was singing, but poetry, lovely poetry, and me and my mother stands gaping up, and all of a tremble. "What is she at all, mother?" says I. "Is it an angel she is, or a faery woman, or what?" With that up come Miss Letty, that was your grandmother, dear, but Miss Letty she was then, and no word of her being anything else, and she wondered to see us gaping up that way, till me and my mother told her of it. She went on gay-dressed then, and was lovely-looking. She was up the lane where none of us could see her coming forward when the Wee Woman rose up in that queer way, saying, "Here comes Miss Letty in all her finery." Who knows to what far country she went, or to see whom dying?

'It was never after dark she came, but daylight always, as far as I mind, but wanst, and that was on a Hallow Eve night. My mother was by the fire, making ready the supper; she had a duck down and some apples. In slips the Wee Woman. "I'm come to pass my Hallow Eve with you," says she. "That's right," says my mother, and thinks to herself, "I can give her her supper nicely." Down she sits by the fire a while. "Now I'll tell you where you'll bring my supper," says she. "In the room beyond there beside the loom—set a chair in and a plate." "When ye're spending the night, mayn't ye as well sit by the table and eat with the rest of us?" "Do what you're bid, and set whatever you give me in the room beyant. I'll eat there and nowhere else." So my mother sets her a plate of duck and some apples, whatever was going, in where she bid, and we got to our supper and she to hers; and when we rose I went in, and there, lo and behold ye, was her supper-plate a bit ate of each portion, and she clean gone!'

1897.

DREAMS THAT HAVE NO MORAL

THE FRIEND who heard about Maeve and the hazel-stick went to the workhouse another day. She found the old people cold and wretched, 'like flies in winter', she said: but they forgot the cold when they began to talk. A man had just left them who had played cards in a rath with the people of Faery, who had played 'very fair'; and one old man had seen an enchanted black pig one night, and there were two old people my friend had heard quarrelling as to whether Raftery or Callanan was the better poet. One had said of Raftery, 'He was a big man, and his songs have gone through the whole world. I remember him well. He had a voice like the wind'; but the other was certain 'that you would stand in the snow to listen to Callanan.' Presently an old man began to tell my friend a story, and all listened delightedly, bursting into laughter now and then. The story, which I am going to tell just as it was told, was one of those old rambling moralless tales, which are the delight of the poor and the hard-driven, wherever life is left in its natural simplicity. They tell of a time when nothing had consequences, when even if you were killed, if only you had a good heart, somebody would bring you to life again with a touch of a rod, and when if you were a prince and happened to look exactly like your brother, you might go to bed with his queen, and have only a little quarrel afterwards. We too, if we were so weak and poor that everything threatened us with misfortune, might remember every old dream that has been strong enough to fling the weight of the world from its shoulders.

The fish and those who ate it

142

There was a king one time who was very much put out because he had no son, and he went at last to consult his chief adviser. And the chief adviser said, 'It's easy enough managed if you do as I tell you. Let you send someone,' says he, 'to such a place to catch a fish. And when the fish is brought in, give it to the queen, your wife, to eat.'

So the king sent as he was told, and the fish was caught and brought in, and he gave it to the cook, and bade her put it before the fire, but to be careful with it, and not to let any blob or blister rise on it. But it is impossible to cook a fish before the fire without the skin of it rising in some place or other, and so there came a blob on the skin, and the cook put her finger on it to smooth it down, and then she put her finger into her mouth to cool it, and so she got a taste of the fish. And then it was sent up to the queen, and she ate it, and what was left of it was thrown out into the yard and there were a mare in the yard and a greyhound, and they ate the bits that were thrown out.

And before the year was out, the queen had a young son, and the cook had a young son, and the mare had two foals, and the greyhound had two pups.

And the two young sons were sent out for a while to some place to be cared, and when they came back they were so much like to one another no person could know which was the queen's son and which was the cook's. And the queen was vexed at that, and she went to the chief adviser and said, 'Tell me some way that I can know which is my own son, for I don't like to be giving the same eating and drinking to the cook's son as to my own.' 'It is easy to know that,' said the chief adviser, 'if you will do as I tell you. Go you outside, and stand at the door they will be coming in by, and when they see you, your own son will bow his head, but the cook's son will only laugh.'

So she did that, and when her own son bowed his head, her servants put a mark on him that she would know him again. And when they were all sitting at their dinner after that, she said to Jack, that was the cook's son, 'It is time for you to go away out of this, for you are not my son.' And her own son, that we will call Bill, said, 'Do not send him away, are we not brothers?' But Jack said, 'I would have been long ago out of this house if I knew it was not my own father and mother owned it.' And for all Bill could say to him, he would not stop. But before he went, they were by the well that was in the garden, and he said to Bill, 'If harm ever happens to me, that water on the top of the well will be blood, and the water below will be honey.'

Then he took one of the pups, and one of the two horses that were foaled after the mare eating the fish, and the wind that was after him could not catch him, and he caught the wind that was before him. And he went on till he came to a weaver's house, and he asked him for a lodging, and he gave it to him. And then he went on till he came to a king's house, and he sent in at the door to ask, 'Did he want a servant?' 'All I want,' said the king, 'is a boy that will drive out the cows to the field every morning, and bring them in at night to be milked.' 'I will do that for you,' said Jack; so the king engaged him.

In the morning Jack was sent out with the four-and-twenty cows, and the place he was told to drive them to had not a blade of grass in it for them, but was full of stones. So Jack looked about for some place where there would be better grass, and after a while he saw a field with good green grass in it, and it belonging to a giant. So he knocked down a bit of the wall and drove them in, and he went up himself into an apple-tree and began to eat the apples. Then the giant came into the field. 'Fee-faw-fum,' says he, 'I smell the blood of an Irishman. I see you where you are, up in the tree,' he said; 'you are too big for one mouthful, and too small for two mouthfuls, and I don't know what I'll do with you if I don't grind you up and make snuff for my nose.' 'As you are strong, be merciful,' says Jack up in the tree. 'Come down out of that, you little dwarf,' said the giant, 'or I'll tear you and the tree asunder.' So Jack came down. 'Would you sooner be driving red-hot knives into one another's hearts,' said the giant, 'or would you sooner be fighting one another on red-hot flags?' 'Fighting on red-hot flags is what I'm used to at home,' said Jack, 'and your dirty feet will be sinking in them and my feet will be rising.' So then they began the fight. The ground that was hard they made soft, and the ground that was soft they made hard, and they made spring wells come up through the green flags. They were like that all through the day, no one getting the upper hand of the other, and at last a little bird came and sat on the bush and said to Jack, 'If you don't make an end of him by sunset, he'll make an end of you.' Then Jack put out his strength, and he brought the giant down on his knees. 'Give me my life,' says the giant, 'and I'll give you the best gift that I have.' 'What is that?' said Jack. 'A sword that nothing can stand against.' 'Where is it to be found?' said Jack. 'In that red door you see there in the hill.' So Jack went and got it out. 'Where will I try the sword?' says he. 'Try it on that ugly black stump of a tree,' says the giant. 'I see nothing blacker or uglier than your own head,' says Jack. And with that he made one stroke, and cut off the giant's head that it went into the air, and he caught it on the sword as it was coming down, and made two halves of it. 'It is well for you I did not join the body again,' said the head, 'or you would have never been able to strike it off again.' 'I did not give you the chance of that,' said Jack.

So he brought the cows home at evening, and every one wondered at all the milk they gave that night. And when the king was sitting at dinner with the princess, his daughter, and the rest, he said, 'I think I only hear two roars from beyond to-night in place of three.'

The next morning Jack went out again with the cows, and he saw another field full of grass, and he knocked down the wall and let the cows in. All happened the same as the day before, but the giant that came this time had two heads, and they fought together, and the little bird came and spoke to Jack as before. And when Jack had brought the giant down, he said, 'Give me my life, and I'll give you the best thing I have.' 'What is that?' says Jack. 'It's a suit that you can put on, and you will see every one but no one can see you.' 'Where is it?' said Jack. 'It's inside that little red door at the side of the hill.' So Jack went and brought out the suit. And then he cut off the giant's two heads, and caught them coming down and made four halves of them. And they said it was well for him he had not given them time to join the body.

That night when the cows came home they gave so much milk that all the vessels that could be found were filled up.

The next morning Jack went out again, and all happened as before, and the giant this time had four heads, and Jack made eight halves of them. And the giant had told him to go to a little blue door in the side of the hill, and there he got a pair of shoes that when you put them on would go faster than the wind.

That night the cows gave so much milk that there were not vessels enough to hold it, and it was given to tenants and to poor people passing the road, and the rest was thrown out at the windows. I was passing that way myself, and I got a drink of it.

That night the king said to Jack, 'Why is it the cows are giving so much milk these days? Are you bringing them to any other grass?' 'I am not,' said Jack, 'but I have a good stick, and whenever they would stop still or lie down, I give them blows of it, that they jump and leap over walls and stones and ditches; that's the way to make cows give plenty of milk.'

And that night at the dinner, the king said, 'I hear no roars at all.'

The next morning, the king and the princess were watching at the window to see what would Jack do when he got to the field. And Jack knew they were there, and he got a stick, and began to batter the cows, that they went leaping and jumping over stones, and walls, and ditches. 'There is no lie in what Jack said,' said the king then.

Now there was a great serpent at that time used to come every seven years, and he had to get a king's daughter to eat, unless she would have some good man to fight for her. And it was the princess at the place Jack was had to be given to it that time, and the king had been feeding a bully underground for seven years, and you may believe he got the best of everything, to be ready to fight it.

And when the time came, the princess went out and the bully with her down to the shore, and when they got there what did he do, but to tie the princess to a tree, the way the serpent would be able to swallow her easy with no delay, and he himself went and hid up in an ivy-tree. And Jack knew what was going on, for the princess had told him about it, and had asked would he help her, but he said he would not. But he came out now, and he put on the sword he had taken from the first giant, and he came by the place the princess was, but she didn't know him. 'Is that right for a princess to be tied to a tree?'' said Jack. 'It is not, indeed,' said she, and she told him what had happened, and how the serpent was coming to take her. 'If you will let me sleep for a while with my head in your lap,' said Jack, 'you could wake me when it is coming.' So he did that, and she awakened him when she saw the serpent coming, and Jack got up and fought with it, and drove it back into the sea. And then he cut the rope that fastened her, and he went away. The bully came down then out of the tree, and he brought the princess to where the king was, and he said, 'I got a friend of mine to come and fight the serpent to-day, when I was a little timorous after being so long shut up underground, but I'll do the fighting myself to-morrow.'

The next day they went out again, and the same thing happened; the bully tied up the princess where the serpent could come at her fair and easy, and went up himself to hide in the ivy-tree. Then Jack put on the suit he had taken from the second giant, and he walked out, and the princess did not know him, but she told him all that had happened yesterday, and how some young gentleman she did not know had come and saved her. So Jack asked might he lie down and take a sleep with his head in her lap, the way she could awake him. And all happened the same way as the day before. And the bully gave her up to the king, and said he had brought another of his friends to fight for her that day.

The next day she was brought down to the shore as before,

The princess, Jack, the serpent and the bully

and a great many people gathered to see the serpent that was coming to bring the king's daughter away. And Jack and the princess had talked as before. But when he was asleep this time, she thought she would make sure of being able to find him again, and she took out her scissors and cut off a piece of his hair, and made a little packet of it and put it away. And she did another thing, she took off one of the shoes that were on his feet.

And when she saw the serpent coming she woke him, and he said, 'This time I will put the serpent in a way that he will eat no more king's daughters.' So he took out the sword he had got from the giant, and he put it in at the back of the serpent's neck, the way blood and water came spouting out that went for fifty miles inland, and made an end of him. And then he made off, and no one saw what way he went, and the bully brought the princess to the king, and claimed to have saved her, and it is he who was made much of, and was the right-hand man after that.

But when the feast was made ready for the wedding, the princess took out the bit of hair she had, and she said she would marry no one but the man whose hair would match that, and she showed the shoe and said that she would marry no one whose foot would not fit that shoe as well. And the bully tried to put on the shoe, but so much as his toe would not go into it, and as to his hair, it didn't match at all to the bit of hair she had cut from the man that saved her.

So then the king gave a great ball, to bring all the chief men of the country together to try would the shoe fit any of them. And they were all going to carpenters and joiners getting bits of their feet cut off to try could they wear the shoe, but it was no use, not one of them could get it on.

Then the king went to his chief adviser and asked what could he do. And the chief adviser bade him to give another ball, and this time he said, 'Give it to poor as well as rich.'

So the ball was given, and many came flocking to it, but the shoe would not fit any one of them. And the chief adviser said, 'Is every one here that belongs to the house?' 'They are all here,' said the king, 'except the boy that minds the cows, and I would not like him to be coming up here.'

Jack was below in the yard at the time, and he heard what the king said, and he was very angry, and he went and got his sword and came running up the stairs to strike off the king's head, but the man that kept the gate met him on the stairs before he could get to the king, and quieted him down, and when he got to the top of the stairs and the princess saw him, she gave a cry and ran into his arms. And they tried the shoe and it fitted him, and his hair matched to the piece that had been cut off. So then they were married, and a great feast was given for three days and three nights.

And at the end of that time, one morning there came a deer outside the window, with bells on it, and they ringing. And it called out, 'Here is the hunt, where are the huntsmen and the hounds?' So when Jack heard that he got up and took his horse and his hound and went hunting the deer. When it was in the hollow he was on the hill, and when it was on the hill he was in the hollow, and that went on all through the day, and when night fell it went into a wood. And Jack went into the wood after it, and all he could see was a mud-wall cabin, and he went in, and there he saw an old woman, about two hundred years old, and she sitting over the fire. 'Did you see a deer pass this way?' says Jack. 'I did not,' says she, 'but it's too late now for you to be following a deer, let you stop the night here.' 'What will I do with my horse and my hound?' said Jack. 'Here are two ribs of hair,' says she, 'and let you tie them up with them.' So Jack went out and tied up the horse and the hound, and when he came in again the old woman said, 'You killed my three sons, and I'm going to kill you now,' and she put on a pair of boxing-gloves, each one of them nine stone weight, and the nails in them fifteen inches long. Then they began to fight, and Jack was getting the worst of it. 'Help, hound!' he cried out, then 'Squeeze, hair!' cried out the old woman, and the rib of hair that was about the hound's neck squeezed him to death. 'Help, horse!' Jack called out, then 'Squeeze, hair!' called out the old woman, and the rib of hair that was about the horse's neck began to tighten and squeeze him to death. Then the old woman made an end of Jack and threw him outside the door.

To go back now to Bill. He was out in the garden one day, and he took a look at the well, and what did he see but the water at the top was blood, and what was underneath was honey. So he went into the house again, and he said to his mother, 'I will never eat a second meal at the same table, or sleep a second night in the same bed, till I know what is happening to Jack.'

So he took the other horse and hound then, and set off, over hills where cock never crows and horn never sounds, and the Devil never blows his bugle. And at last he came to the weaver's house, and when he went in, the weaver says, 'You are welcome, and I can give you better treatment than I did the last time you came in to me,' for he thought it was Jack who was there, they were so much like one another. 'That is good,' said Bill to himself, 'my brother has been here.' And he gave the weaver the full of a basin of gold in the morning before he left.

Then he went on till he came to the king's house and when he was at the door the princess came running down the stairs, and said, 'Welcome to you back again.' And all the people said, 'It is a wonder you have gone hunting three days after your marriage, and to stop so long away.' So he stopped that night with the princess, and she thought it was her own husband all the time.

And in the morning the deer came, and bells ringing on it, under the windows, and called out, 'The hunt is here, where are the huntsmen and the hounds?' Then Bill got up and got his horse and his hound, and followed it over hills and hollows till they came to the wood, and there he saw nothing but the mud-wall cabin and the old woman sitting by the fire, and she bade him stop the night there, and gave him two ribs of hair to tie his horse and his hound with. But Bill was wittier than Jack was, and before he went out, he threw the ribs of hair into the fire secretly. When he came in the old woman said, 'Your brother killed my three sons, and I killed him, and I'll kill you along with him.' And she put her gloves on, and they began to fight, and then Bill called out, 'Help, horse!' 'Squeeze hair!' called the old woman. 'I can't squeeze, I'm in the fire,' said the hair. And the horse came in and gave her a blow of his hoof. 'Help, hound!' said Bill then. 'Squeeze hair!' said the old woman. 'I can't squeeze, I'm in the fire,' said the second hair. Then the hound put his teeth in her, and Bill brought her down, and she cried for mercy. 'Give me my life,' she said, 'and I'll tell you where you'll get your brother again, and his hound and horse.' 'Where's that?' said Bill. 'Do you see that rod over the fire?' said she; 'take it down and go outside the door where you'll see three green stones, and strike them with the rod, for they are your brother, and his horse and hound, and they'll come to life again.' 'I will, but I'll make a green stone of you first,' said Bill, and he cut off her head with his sword.

Then he went out and struck the stones, and sure enough there were Jack and his horse and hound, alive and well. And they began striking other stones around, and men came from them, that had been turned to stones, hundreds and thousands of them.

Then they set out for home, but on the way they had some dispute or some argument together, for Jack was not well pleased to hear he had spent the night with his wife, and Bill got angry, and he struck Jack with the rod, and turned him to a green stone. And he went home, but the princess saw he had something on his mind, and he said then, 'I have killed my brother.' And he went back then and brought him to life, and they lived happy ever after, and they had children by the basketful, and threw them out by the shovelful. I was passing one time myself, and they called me in and gave me a cup of tea.

1902.

BY THE ROADSIDE

LAST NIGHT I went to a wide place on the Kiltartan road to listen to some Irish songs. While I waited for the singers an old man sang about that country beauty who died so many years ago, and spoke of a singer he had known who sang so beautifully that no horse would pass him, but must turn its head and cock its ears to listen. Presently a score of men and boys and girls, with shawls over their heads, gathered under the trees to listen. Somebody sang *Sa Muirnin Díles*, and then somebody else *Jimmy Mo Mílestór*, mournful songs of separation, of death, and of exile. Then some of the men stood up and began to dance, while another lilted the measure they danced to, and then somebody sang *Eiblín a Rúin*, that glad song of meeting which has always moved me more than other songs, because the lover who made it sang it to his sweetheart under the shadow of a mountain I looked at every day through my childhood. The voices melted into the twilight, and were mixed into the trees, and when I thought of the words they too melted away, and were mixed with the generations of men. Now it was a phrase, now it was an attitude of mind, an emotional form, that had carried my memory to older verses, or even to forgotten mythologies. I was carried so far that it was as though I came to one of the four rivers, and followed it under the wall of Paradise to the roots of the Trees of Knowledge and of Life. There is no song or story handed down among the cottages that has not words and thoughts to carry one as far, for though one can know but a little of their ascent, one knows that they ascend like mediaeval genealogies through unbroken dignities to the beginning of the world. Folk-art is, indeed, the oldest of the aristocracies of thought, and because it refuses what is passing and trivial, the merely clever and pretty, as certainly as the vulgar and insincere, and because it has gathered into itself the simplest and most unforgettable thoughts of the generations, it is the soil where all great art is rooted. Wherever it is spoken by the fireside, or sung by the roadside, or carved upon the lintel, appreciation of the arts that a single mind gives unity and design to, spreads quickly when its hour is come.

In a society that has cast out imaginative tradition, only a few people—three or four thousand out of millions—favoured by their own characters and by happy circumstance, and only then after much labour, have understanding of imaginative things, and yet 'the imagination is the man himself.' The Churches in the Middle Ages won all the arts into their service because men understood that when imagination is impoverished, a principal voice—some would say the only voice—for the awakening of wise hope and durable faith, and understanding charity, can speak but in broken words, if it does not fall silent. And so it has always seemed to me that we, who would re-awaken imaginative tradition by making old songs live again, or by gathering old stories into books, take part in the quarrel of Galilee. Those who are Irish and would spread foreign ways, which, for all but a few, are ways of spiritual poverty, take part also. Their part is with those who were of Jewry, and yet cried out, 'If thou let this man go thou art not Caesar's friend.'

1901.

APPENDIX

THE FOUR WINDS OF DESIRE

IN THE NOTES at the end of *Beside the Fire*, Dr. Hyde contrasts with certain tales of Indian jugglery an old Gaelic account of a magician who threw a rope-ladder into the air and then sent climbing up it all manner of men and beasts. It reads like an allegory to explain the charms of folk and faery-tales: a parable to show how man mounts to the infinite by the ladder of the impossible. When our narrow rooms, our short lives, our soon-ended passions and emotions, put us out of conceit with sooty and finite reality, we have only to read some story like Dr. Hyde's 'Paudeen O'Kelly and the Weasel', and listen to the witch complaining to the robber, 'Why did you bring away my gold that I was for five hundred years gathering through the hills and hollows of the world?' Here at last is a universe where all is large and intense enough to satisfy the emotions of man. Certainly such stories are not a criticism of life but rather an extension, thereby much more closely resembling Homer than that last and most admirable phase of 'the improving book', a social drama by Henrik Ibsen. They are as existence and not a thought, and make our world of tea-tables seem but a shabby penumbra.

It is perhaps, therefore, by no means strange that the age of 'realism' should also be the harvest-time of folk-lore. We grow tired of tuning our fiddles to the clank of this our heavy chain, and lay them down to listen gladly to one who tells us of men hundreds of years old and endlessly mirthful. Our new-wakened interest in the impossible has been of the greatest service to Irish folk-literature.

155

Until about five years ago the only writers who had dealt with the subject at any length were Crofton Croker, a second-hand bookseller named Kennedy, and an anonymous writer in *The Dublin and London Magazine* for 1825 and 1828. Others, it is true, had incorporated (like Gerald Griffin) odd folk-tales in the pages of long novels, or based on them (like Carleton and Lover) stories of peasant life. Croker was certainly no ideal collector. He altered his materials without word or warning, and could never resist the chance of turning some naïve faery tale into a drunken peasant's dream. With all his buoyant humour and imagination he was continually guilty of that great sin against art—the sin of rationalism. He tried to take away from his stories the impossibility that makes them dear to us. Nor could he quite desist from dressing his personages in the dirty rags of the stage Irishman. Kennedy, an incomparably worse writer, had one great advantage: he believed in his goblins as sincerely as any peasant. He has explained in his *Legendary Fictions* that he could tell a number of spells for raising the faeries, but he will not—for fear of putting his readers up to mischief. Years went by, and it seemed that we should never have another gathering. Then about five years ago came Lady Wilde's two volumes, and David Fitzgerald's contributions to the *Revue Celtique*; with M'Anally's inaccurate and ill-written *Irish Wonders*, and Curtin's fine collection a little later; and now appears Dr. Hyde's incomparable book. There has been published in five years as much Irish folk-lore as in the foregoing fifty. Its quality, too, is higher. Dr. Hyde's volume is the best written of any. He has caught and faithfully reproduced the peasant idiom and phrase. In becoming scientifically accurate, he has not ceased to be a man of letters. His fifteen translations from traditional Gaelic originals are models of what such translations should be. Unlike Campbell of Islay, he has not been content merely to turn the Gaelic into English; but where the idiom is radically different he has searched out colloquial equivalents from among the English-speaking peasants. The Gaelic is printed side by side with the English, so that the substantial accuracy

of his versions can always be tested. The result is many pages
in which you can hear in imagination the very voice of the
sennachie, and almost smell the smoke of his turf fire.

Now and then Dr. Hyde has collected stories which he was
compelled to write out in his own Irish through the impossibility, he tells us, of taking them down word for word at the
time. He has only printed a half of one story of this kind
in *Beside the Fire*. One wishes he had not been so rigorous
in the matter, especially as it is for this reason, I conclude,
that *Teig O'Kane*, still the weirdest of Irish folk-tales, has
been printed elsewhere but one would gladly have his stories
under one cover. He is so completely a Gael, alike in thought
and literary idiom, that I do not think he could falsify a
folk-tale if he tried. At the most he would change it as a few
years' passing from sennachie to sennachie must do perforce.
Two villages a mile apart will have the same story; why, then,
should Dr. Hyde exclude his own reverent adoptions? We
cannot all read them in the Gaelic of his *Leabhar Sgeul-
aighteachta*. Is it the evil communications of that very
scientific person, Mr. Alfred Nutt (he contributes learned
notes), which have robbed us of the latter pages of *Guleesh
na Guss Dhu?* We might have at least had some outline of the
final adventures of the young faery seer and the French
princess. After all, imaginative impulse—the quintessence of
life—is our great need from folk-lore. When we have
banqueted let Learning gather the crumbs into her larder, and
welcome. She will serve them up again in time of famine.

Dr. Hyde has four tales of hidden treasure, five stories
of adventure with a princess or a fortune at the end, a legend
or a haunted forest at the end, and a tale of a man who grew
very thin and weakly through swallowing a hungry newt,
which was only dislodged when made wildly athirst by a heavy
dinner of salt pork and the allurement of a running stream.
Love, fortune, adventure, wonder—the four winds of desire!
There is also a chapter of quaint riddles in rhyme. The whole
book is full of charming expressions. The French princess is
described as 'the loveliest woman on the edge of the world.
The rose and the lily were fighting together in her face, and

one could not tell which would get the victory.' Here and there, too, is a piece of delicate observation, as when Guleesh na Guss Dhu waits for the faeries listening to 'the cronawn (hum) of the insects,' and watching 'the fadoques and fibeens (golden and green clover) rising and lying, lying and rising, as they do on a fine night.' The riddles also have no lack of poetry. Here is a description of a boreen or little country lane:

> 'From house to house he goes,
> A messenger small and slight,
> And whether it rains or snows
> He sleeps outside in the night.'

And here is one of the lintel on a wet day—

> 'There's a poor man at rest,
> With a stick beneath his breast,
> And he breaking his heart a-crying.'

These riddles are the possession of children, and have the simple fancifulness of childhood.

It is small wonder that this book should be beautiful, for it is the chronicle of that world of glory and surprise imagined in the unknown by the peasant as he leant painfully over his spade. His spiritual desires ascended into heaven, but all he could dream of material well-being and freedom was lavished upon this world of kings and goblins. We who have less terrible a need dream less splendidly. Dr. Hyde bids us know that all this exultant world of fancies is passing away, soon to exist for none but stray scholars and the gentlemen of the sun-myth. He has written on his title-page this motto from an old Gaelic poem: 'They are like a mist on the coming of night that is scattered away by a light breath of wind.' I know that this is the common belief of folk-lorists, but I do not feel certain that it is altogether true. Much, no doubt, will perish—perhaps the whole tribe of folk-tales proper; but the faery and ghost kingdom is more stubborn than men dream of. It will perhaps be always going and never gone. I have talked with many who believe they have seen it, and I have had my own glimpse of unaccountable things. Why should Swedenborg alone have visions? Surely the mantle of Coleridge's 'man of ten centuries' is large enough to cover the witch-doctors at any rate. There is not so much difference between them. Swedenborg's assertion, in the *Spiritual Diary*, that 'the angels do not like butter,' would make admirable folk-lore. Dr. Hyde finds a sun-myth in one of his most ancient stories. The sun and the revolving seasons have not yet done helping to draw legends from the right minds. Some time ago a friend of mine talked with an old Irish peasant who had seen a vision of a great tree, amid whose branches two animals, one white and one black, pursued each other continually; and wherever the white beast came the branches burst into foliage, and wherever the black one, then all withered away. The changing of the seasons, among the rest, is here very palpable. Only let it be quite plain that the peasant's vision meant much more than the mere atmosphere allegory of the learned. He saw within his tree the birth and death of all things. It cast a light of imagination on his own dull cattle-minding and earth-turning destiny, and gave him heart to repeat the Gaelic proverb—'The lake is not burdened by its swan, a steed by its bridle, or a man by the soul that is in him.'

Into the Twilight

Out-worn heart, in a time out-worn,
Come clear of the nets of wrong and right;
Laugh, heart, again in the grey twilight;
Sigh, heart, again in the dew of the morn.

Your mother Eire is always young,
Dew ever shining and twilight grey;
Though hope fall from you and love decay,
Burning in fires of a slanderous tongue.

Come, heart, where hill is heaped upon hill:
For there the mystical brotherhood
Of sun and moon and hollow and wood
And river and stream work out their will;

And God stands winding His lonely horn,
And time and the world are ever in flight;
And love is less kind than the grey twilight,
And hope is less dear than the dew of the morn.

THE END